School Committee Boston (Mass.)

Rules of the School Committee

And Regulations of the Public Schools of the City of Boston

School Committee Boston (Mass.)

Rules of the School Committee
And Regulations of the Public Schools of the City of Boston

ISBN/EAN: 9783337159467

Printed in Europe, USA, Canada, Australia, Japan

Cover: Foto ©Suzi / pixelio.de

More available books at **www.hansebooks.com**

RULES

OF

THE SCHOOL COMMITTEE,

AND

REGULATIONS OF THE PUBLIC SCHOOLS

OF THE

CITY OF BOSTON.

BOSTON:
J. E. FARWELL AND COMPANY, PRINTERS TO THE CITY,
37 CONGRESS STREET.
1865.

SCHOOL COMMITTEE.

THE following special provisions in regard to the number of the School Committee, the manner in which they shall be chosen, their terms of service, and their powers and duties, are contained in the City Charter, from which the following Sections are copied : —

"SECT. 53. The School Committee shall consist of the Mayor of the city, the President of the Common Council, and of the persons hereinafter mentioned. A majority of the persons duly elected shall constitute a quorum for the transaction of business ; and at all meetings of the Board the Mayor, if present, shall preside. *School Committee.*

"SECT. 54. At the annual election next after the passage of this act, the qualified voters of each ward shall be called upon to give in their ballots for six inhabitants of the ward, to be members of the School Committee ; and the two persons who receive the highest number of votes, or in case more than two receive an equal number of votes, the two persons who are senior by age, shall hold their office for three years from the second Monday in January next ensuing, and the next two persons who receive the highest number of votes, or who are senior by age in the contingency aforesaid, shall hold their office for two years from said date, and the two other persons shall hold their office for one year from said date ; and at every subsequent annual election, two persons shall be chosen in each ward, to be members of the School Committee for the term of three years. *Election of School Committee.*

"SECT. 55. The persons so chosen as members of the School Committee, shall meet and organize on the second Monday of January, at such hour as the Mayor may appoint. They may choose a secretary and such subordinate officers as they may deem expedient, and shall define their duties, and fix their respective salaries. *Organization of School Committee.*

Duties of School Committee.

"SECT. 56. The said Committee shall have the care and management of the public schools, and may elect all such instructors as they may deem proper, and remove the same whenever they consider it expedient. And generally they shall have all the powers in relation to the care and management of the public schools, which the selectmen of towns or school committees are authorized by the laws of this Commonwealth to exercise."

Elections.

"SECT. 24. The Board of Aldermen, the Common Council, and the School Committee, shall have authority to decide upon all questions relative to the qualifications, elections, and returns of their respective members."

Vacancies, &c.

The General Statutes, chapter 38, contain the following provisions concerning vacancies in School Committees: —

"SECTION 17. If any person elected a member of the School Committee, after being duly notified of his election in the manner in which town officers are required to be notified, refuses or neglects to accept said office, or if any member of the board declines further service, or, from change of residence or otherwise, becomes unable to attend to the duties of the Board, the remaining members shall, in writing, give notice of the fact to the selectmen of the town, or to the Mayor and Aldermen of the city, and the two Boards shall thereupon, after giving public notice of at least one week, proceed to fill such vacancy; and a majority of the ballots of persons entitled to vote shall be necessary to an election.

SECT. 18. If all the persons elected as members of the School Committee, after such notice of their election, refuse or neglect to accept the office, or, having accepted, afterwards decline further service, or become unable to attend to the duties of the Board, the selectmen or the Mayor and aldermen shall, after giving like public notice, proceed by ballot to elect a new Board, and the votes of a majority of the entire board of selectmen, or of the Mayor and Aldermen, shall be necessary to an election.

SECT. 19. The term of service of every member elected in pursuance of the provisions of the two preceding sections, shall end with the municipal or official year in which he is chosen; and if the vacancy which he was elected to fill was for a longer period, it shall, at the first annual election after the occurrence of the vacancy, be filled in the manner prescribed for original elections of the School Committee.

RULES

BOARD OF SCHOOL COMMITTEE.

CHAPTER I.

Organization of the Board.

SECTION 1.   At all meetings of the Board of School Committee, the Mayor, styled President, shall preside ; in his absence, the President of the Common Council shall preside ; and in the absence of both the Mayor and President of the Common Council, a President *pro tempore* shall be chosen by ballot. {Organization of the Board.}

SECT. 2.   At the first meeting in each year, the Board shall elect a Secretary by ballot, and fix his salary for the ensuing year ; and the President shall appoint, subject to the approval of the Board, the following Standing Committees of five members each, viz : 1. On Elections ; — 2. On Rules and Regulations ; — 3. On Accounts ; — 4. On Schoolhouses ; — 5. On Salaries ; — 6. On Text-Books ; — 7. On Music ; — 8. On Printing ; — * and the following, of thirteen members each, one member to be selected from each of the twelve wards of the city, viz : 1. On the Latin School ; — 2. On the English High School ; — 3. On the Girls' High and Normal School. {Standing Committees.}

SECT. 3.   For convenience in the management of the Grammar and Primary Schools, the city shall be divided into as many Districts as it has Grammar Schools : each District shall take its name from the Grammar School {Districts.}

* See note on page 14.

District Committees.

within its boundaries; the President shall appoint, at the first meeting of the Board in each year, and subject to its approval, a Standing Committee on each District, whose number, in each case, shall be proportionate to the number of schools in the District.

Chairmen of sub-committees.

SECT. 4. The member first named on any committee, shall be the chairman thereof; except that the Committee on the Latin School, on the English High School, on the Girls' High and Normal School, and each District Committee, shall respectively elect its own chairman.

Annual and quarterly meetings.

SECT. 5. The Board shall hold its annual meeting for the election of teachers on the second Tuesday in June, and three other stated quarterly meetings on the second Tuesday in March, September, and December, at seven and a half o'clock, P. M., at such place as the President may appoint; and the Board may hold special meetings whenever they are deemed necessary.

Quorum.

SECT. 6. For a quorum, a majority of the Board must be present; but a less number may vote to send for absent members, and to adjourn. Whenever the Board is obliged to wait, after the hour appointed for the meeting, for a quorum to begin business, or whenever it has to suspend business and adjourn for want of a quorum, the roll shall be called and the names of the absentees recorded by the Secretary.

Vacancies in the Board.

SECT. 7. Whenever a vacancy occurs in this Board, a Committee shall be appointed, consisting of three members from the ward in which the vacancy exists, and two at large, who shall consult with the Aldermen of said ward, or with the Chairman of the Board of Aldermen, in case the ward is not represented in that branch, and report to this Board, on or before the day of election, the name of a suitable candidate to fill said vacancy.

CHAPTER II.

Powers and Duties of the President.

SECTION 1.   The President shall take the chair pre- Opening of meetings. cisely at the hour appointed for the meeting of the Board, and shall call the members to order, and, on the appearance of a quorum, he shall cause the records of the last meeting to be read, and shall proceed to business in the following order, and shall not depart from it unless authorized by a vote of the Board.

1. Papers from the City Council :   Order of business.
2. Unfinished business of preceding meetings ;
3. Nomination and Confirmation of Teachers ;
4. Reports of Committees :
5. Motions, Orders, Resolutions, Petitions, &c.

The Nomination and Confirmation of Teachers shall be called for in the order of the districts.

SECT. 2.   The President shall preserve order and Duties of the President. decorum in the meetings ; he may speak to points of order in preference to other members, and shall decide all questions of order, subject to an appeal to the Board, on motion of any member regularly seconded, and no other business shall be in order till the question on the appeal shall have been decided.

SECT. 3.   When two or more members rise to speak same. at the same time, the President shall name the member who may speak first.

SECT. 4.   He shall rise to address the Board, and to same. put a question, but may read sitting.   He shall declare all votes ; but if any member doubt the vote, the President, without debate, shall require the members voting to rise and stand until they are counted, and he shall declare the result.

Committee of the Whole. Sect. 5. The President shall appoint the chairman when the Board goes into Committee of the Whole; at any other time he may call any member to the chair, but such substitution shall not continue longer than one meeting. He may express his opinion on any subject under debate; but in such case, he shall leave the chair, and shall not resume it while the same question is pending; but he may state facts, and give his opinion on questions of order, without leaving his place.

Yeas and nays. Sect. 6. The President shall take the sense of the Board by *Yeas* and *Nays*, whenever *one fifth* of the members present sustain a motion therefor.

Motions. Sect. 7. All questions shall be propounded by the President in the order in which they are moved, unless the subsequent motion shall be previous in its nature; except that in naming sums and fixing times, the largest sum and the longest time shall be put first. After a motion is seconded, and stated by the President, it shall be disposed of by vote of the Board, unless the mover withdraw it before a decision or an amendment.

Motion to adjourn. Sect. 8. The President shall consider a motion to adjourn as always in order, except when a member has the floor, or when a question has been put and not decided; and motions to adjourn, to lay upon the table, to take from the table, and for the previous question, shall be decided without debate. Any member who moves to adjourn to a day certain, shall assign his reasons for so doing.

Previous question. Sect. 9. He shall put the previous question in the following form: "Shall the main question be now put?" and all debate shall be suspended until the previous question shall have been decided. The adoption of the previous question shall put an end to all debate, to bring the Board to a direct vote upon pending amendments, if any, in their regular order, and then upon the main question.

Sect. 10.   Whenever in his opinion it is necessary, Call of special meetings. the President *may*, and at the written request of any five members, he *shall* call a special meeting of the Board; but no meeting of the Board shall be called on shorter notice than twenty-four hours.

Sect. 11.   All Committees shall be nominated by Appointment of committees. the President, unless otherwise ordered by the Board.

CHAPTER III.

Rights and Duties of Members.

Section 1.   When any member is about to speak in Duties of members in debate. debate, or to present any matter to the Board, he shall rise in his place, and respectfully address the President; shall confine himself to the question under debate, and avoid personality.   No member in debate shall mention another by his name, but may describe him by the ward he represents, the place he sits in, or such other designation as may be intelligible and respectful.

Sect. 2.   No member while speaking shall be inter- Call to order. rupted by another, but by rising to call to order, or to correct a mistake.   But if any member, in speaking or otherwise, transgress the rules of the Board, the President *shall*, or any member *may*, call him to order; in which case the member so called to order shall immediately sit down, unless permitted to explain; and the Board, if appealed to, shall decide on the case, but without debate.

Sect. 3.   If the Board shall determine that a mem- Violation of Rules. ber has violated any of its Rules, he shall not be allowed

B

to speak unless by way of excuse for the same, until he shall have made satisfaction therefor.

Rules of debate.   SECT. 4. No member shall speak more than twice to the same question, without leave of the Board; nor more than once until all other members choosing to speak shall have spoken.

Motions.   SECT. 5. No motion shall be considered by the Board unless seconded. Every motion shall be submitted in writing, if the President direct, or any other member of the Board request it.

Order of motions.   SECT. 6. When a question is under debate, no motion shall be received but to adjourn; to lay on the table; for the previous question; to postpone to a day certain; to commit; to amend; or to postpone indefinitely; which several motions shall have precedence in the order above stated.

Reconsideration.   SECT. 7. When a question has once been decided, any member voting in the majority may move a reconsideration; such motion, if made at the same meeting with the decision, shall prevail if a majority of the members present sustain it; but if made at the subsequent meeting, it shall not prevail unless a majority of the whole Board vote for it; and only *one* motion for the reconsideration of any vote shall be permitted.

Members to vote.   SECT. 8. Every member present when a question is put, shall give his vote unless excused by the Board.

SECT. 9. All motions and reports may be committed and recommitted at the pleasure of the Board.

Division of a question.   SECT. 10. The division of a question may be called for, when the sense will admit of it.

Reading of a paper, when called for.   SECT. 11. When the reading of a paper is called for, and the same is objected to by any member, it shall be determined by a vote of the Board.

Suspension of Rules.   SECT. 12. The consent of *three fourths* of the members present at any meeting shall be requisite for the suspension of any standing Rule of the Board, or Regulation of the Schools, unless the proposal for the same shall have lain upon the table for at least one week.

SECT. 13. Whenever any proposition is submitted by a member to amend or repeal any Rule of the Board, or involving the amendment or repeal of any Regulation of the Public Schools, said proposition, before any action thereon, shall be referred to the Committee on Rules and Regulations, or to such other committee, standing or special, as the Board may designate, who shall report thereupon, in writing, and said report, together with such recommendations or orders as may be therein contained, shall be open to immediate consideration and action. *Repeal or amendment of Rules.*

CHAPTER IV.
Duties of Standing Committees.

SECTION 1. Immediately after the appointment of the Standing Committees, at the meeting for organization, the Committee on Elections shall receive the certificates of election of the members, and examine them, and report the result of their examination without any unnecessary delay. Whenever any person shall be elected to fill any vacancy that may have occurred in the Board, this Committee shall examine his certificate of election, and report as above provided, and said committee shall hear and report on all cases of contested elections. *Committee on Elections.*

SECT. 2. The Committee on Rules and Regulations shall take into careful consideration every proposition presented to the Board, to repeal or to amend any Rule or Regulation, whenever the same shall be referred to them, and shall report in writing, stating their reasons for or against the proposed alteration. *Committee on Rules and Regulations.*

Committee on
Accounts.

SECT. 3.   Whenever any proposition is submitted to this Board, involving the payment of money for any other purpose than the payment of salaries, or the establishment of a new school, such proposition shall not be acted upon before it has been referred to the Committee on accounts. Said Committee shall have power to authorize the purchase of all stationery, record books, and blanks for the use of the schools, and a further supply, when called for, of any apparatus, globes, maps, or books of reference, or other conveniences, which this Board may have authorized the use of as means of illustrating the studies of the school. No Sub-Committee, nor any other persons connected with this Board, shall expend any money for these supplies, without authority from this Committee, and no bills for such expenditures shall be paid without the signature of the Chairman of this Committee in approval. Said Committee are authorized, on behalf of this Board, to carry out the provisions of the statute of the Commonwealth for furnishing books to indigent children and others, and to present an estimate of the expenses of the Public Schools to the City Auditor on or before the first day of February annually.*

Mover of a motion, &c., to be notified of the time of its consideration.

SECT. 4.   Whenever a motion, order, or resolution shall be referred to a Committee, the Chairman of the Committee shall cause the member offering the motion, order, or resolution, to be notified by the Secretary of the Board, or otherwise, of the time when the subject will be considered.

Committee on Schoolhouses.

SECT. 5.   Whenever any application shall be made for the erection or alteration of a schoolhouse, such application shall be referred to the Committee on School-

---

* The School Committee shall present to the Auditor, on or before the first day of February in each year, an estimate, in writing, of the expenses of the public schools for the next financial year, stating the amount required for salaries, for incidental expenses, and for the alteration, repair, and erection of schoolhouses. [City Ordinance, December 18, 1855, sect. 2.]

houses, who shall consider the same, and shall consult with the District Committee who may have charge of the school or schools to be accommodated, and shall report to this Board, in writing, such recommendations in each case as they may deem expedient. It shall, also be the duty of the Committee on Schoolhouses to exercise a Warming and general supervision over the warming and ventilation of ventilation of schoolhouses. the several schoolhouses throughout the year.

SECT. 6. Whenever any proposition is submitted to Committee on Salaries. this Board to extend the salary of any teacher beyond the time of actual service, or to change the regular salary of a teacher in any respect, or to pay for any extra service in teaching, *such* proposition shall not be acted upon before it has been referred to the Committee on Salaries, who shall report, in writing, such recommendations as they may deem expedient.

SECT. 7. The Committee on Text-Books, when Committee on Text-Books. they think favorably of any application made by any author or publisher to introduce any new text-book into the Public Schools, shall give early notice thereof to the Board, and see that such author or publisher furnish every member of the Board with a copy of such text-book for examination, as a condition of its being presented to them for acceptance; and said Committee shall fully consider such application, examine thoroughly such text-book, and at such time as they may be prepared, within three months from the date of the application, they shall make a written report to the Board, setting forth the reasons for or against the introduction of said text-book into the Public Schools. In the month of May, annually, this Committee shall examine the course of studies prescribed for the schools, and shall recommend to the Board, at the quarterly meeting in June, such improvements in the course of instruction,

and such changes in the books used in the schools, as
they may deem expedient.

Introduction of new books. SECT. 8. Whenever any new text-book is adopted
by the Board, it shall be on the condition that the pub-
lisher will furnish copies to the pupils of the Public
Schools at such reduction from the wholesale price as
shall be agreed upon by this Board; and it shall be the
duty of the Committee on Text-Books to see that this
condition is fulfilled, and that said book comes into use
at the commencement of the Public Schools after the
August vacation, at which time only shall any new text-
book be introduced.

Committee on Music. SECT. 9. The Committee on Music shall exercise
a general supervision over this department of Public
Instruction in all the schools. They shall appoint,
and nominate to the Board for confirmation, suitably
qualified persons as Teachers of Music;* they shall

---

* *Ordered :* That, in addition to the teachers of music in the Grammar
Schools, the Committee on Music be authorized to nominate to this Board
for confirmation, a suitably qualified person as instructor in Music in the
Primary Schools, with a salary not exceeding twelve hundred dollars per
annum. (Passed June 21, 1864.)

At a meeting of the School Committee, Dec. 27, 1864, the following orders
were passed : —

Ordered : That a standing Committee of five on Gymnastics and Military
Drill be hereafter appointed, whose duty it shall be to enforce the regulations
upon this subject and superintend this branch of instruction, making from
time to time such recommendations to the General Committee as they shall
find expedient.

Ordered : That said Committee be authorized forthwith to employ an Instructor in vocal and physical gymnastics, at a salary not exceeding fifteen
hundred dollars per annum, whose duty it shall be to attend the schools at
such times and for so much of the time as the Committee shall deem necessary,
upon consultation with him and the District Committees, for the purpose of
instructing in gymnastic exercises, both vocal and physical, and of securing the
careful and regular performance of those exercises at such hours as may be
convenient, provided that not less than twenty minutes per day shall be devoted to this purpose in any grammar school, and not less than thirty minutes
in any primary school, in addition to the ordinary recess.

Ordered : That the said Committee, upon consultation with the District
Committees, be also authorized to arrange the Grammar Schools containing

make examinations of each Grammar School in music, at least once in six months, and submit a written report thereupon semi-annually at the quarterly meeting in March and in September.

Sect. 10. The Committee on Printing shall exercise a general supervision in relation to all printing which may be required by the Board, or for any of the Schools under its charge ; and no bill for printing, of any kind, shall be paid without the signature of the Chairman of this Committee, in approval. Said Committee shall submit to this Board, at the quarterly meeting in March, a detailed account of all expenditures for printing during the year preceding. *Committee on Printing.*

Sect. 11. The Committees on the Latin School, the English High School, and the Girls' High and Normal School in all matters relating to said schools and the appointment of teachers therein, shall respectively observe the same rules, and perform the same duties, so far as applicable, as are hereinafter prescribed for the several District Committees in relation to the Grammar Schools under their charge ; and at meetings for the transaction of business, five members shall constitute a quorum. *Committees on High Schools.*

Sect. 12. The member first named on each District Committee shall call a meeting of said Committee within ten days after its appointment. It shall organize by the choice, from among its own members, of a Chairman and Secretary, notice of whose election shall be imme- *Organization of District Committees.*

inale pupils into groups, so that the boys of sufficient size to drill with arms, and in number sufficient to form a military company, may be instructed together in military drill, by a suitable instructor, to be employed by the Committee ; that these companies be united into a larger organization, as the Committee shall find expedient ; and that suitable places and arms be provided by the Committee ; the hours of drill not to exceed two per week, except voluntary drills out of school hours ; and no expenditure exceeding fifteen hundred dollars per annum to be incurred for these purposes without the prior authority of the whole Board.

16

RULES.

[Chap. IV.

diately sent to the Secretary of the School Board. It shall keep a record of its proceedings, and all its official acts shall be done in meetings duly called, at not less than twenty-four hours' notice, and, when reported to the Board, shall be submitted in writing.

Duties of District Committees.
Classification of pupils.

SECT. 13. Each District Committee shall have charge of the Grammar Schools and the Primary Schools in the District, and may arrange the studies and classify the pupils in the latter in such a manner as they may consider most advantageous to the schools. Within ten days after its appointment, each District Committee shall divide itself into a suitable number of Sub-Committees, for the Primary Schools in its District. Said Committee shall then divide the Primary Schools in the District into as many divisions as there may be Sub-Committees, and shall assign each division to a Sub-Committee, who

Care of Primary Schools.

shall have the special charge of the schools in such division; shall visit each of them as often as once in each month; shall examine them quarterly; and shall report, in writing, their standing and progress, to the Chairman of the District Committee, at least one week previous to each quarterly meeting of the Board. Each Sub-Committee shall refer all matters of importance pertaining to the schools under its care, to the District Committee, for consideration and action.

Additional Primary Schools.

SECT. 14. Whenever any District Committee shall deem an additional Primary School necessary for the proper accommodation of the children under their care, they shall state the facts in the case to the Board, in writing, which communication shall be referred to the Committee on Schoolhouses, who shall consider and report on the same before the Board shall take final action on the subject.

Quarterly examinations.

SECT. 15. The District Committee shall examine

the Grammar Schools in their respective Districts at least once in each quarter; and shall visit them not less than once each month, without giving previous notice to the instructors; and shall, at each quarterly meeting of the Board, make a report in writing, giving the results of their examinations and visits, together with the results of the examination by the Sub-Committees of the several Primary Schools under their charge; also stating any occurrences affecting the standing and usefulness of the schools, and mentioning the condition of the schoolhouses and yards and out-buildings connected therewith. They shall also state in their reports whether the rule relating to the infliction of corporal punishment has been complied with; and the names of all children admitted to the schools under their charge who do not reside in the city, and the reasons for their admission.

SECT. 16. At each quarterly meeting, the Chairman of each District Committee, or any member thereof who may be present, shall be called upon for a report on the condition of the schools in the District; and in case of omission to make it, the Board shall pass a vote, enjoining the delinquent Committee to proceed without delay to the performance of their duty, and shall adjourn to receive their report. *Quarterly reports.*

SECT. 17. The District Committee shall determine on the scholars who are to receive the medals and certificates of merit in their respective schools, and return the names to the Secretary, at least four days previous to the annual exhibition. It shall also be their duty, on the day of exhibition, to present the medals and certificates to the pupils to whom they have been awarded. The number of medals and certificates of merit to be awarded in each school, shall be based upon the aver- *Medals and certificates.*

c

age number of pupils belonging to the school during the school year. Each school shall be entitled to one medal and one of each of the certificates of merit for every sixty scholars; and an additional medal may be awarded in any Grammar School in which a majority fraction occurs, if the District Committee deem it expedient. But, in any school where the number of scholars in the first class is comparatively small, the number of medals awarded shall be proportionably less; and it shall never exceed one third of the number of candidates examined, nor shall any pupil be promoted for the purpose of increasing the number of candidates. In any school where there are no scholars much advanced in improvement, no medal shall be awarded. General scholarship, and more especially good conduct, shall be taken into consideration in awarding the medals and certificates; and in order that a just assignment may be made, the District Committee shall critically examine the candidates, and inspect the school records of their standing.

Pupils to attend school in Section where they reside. SECT. 18. No pupil shall be admitted to or retained in any school, except that for the Section in which such pupil resides, without the written consent of the District Committee, both of the school to which the pupil belongs, and of that where he seeks· to be admitted or retained.

Teacher of Sewing. SECT. 19. Instruction shall be given in Sewing to all the pupils in the fourth class in each of the Grammar Schools for girls, except whenever in the judgment of the District Committee it will be for the interest of the school to omit such instruction, in which case the District Committee shall apply to this Board for authority to suspend the action of this rule in that school. The District Committee of each school in which such instruction shall be given shall nominate to this Board, for confirmation, some qualified person as Teacher of Sewing, who shall give to each pupil two lessons of not less than one hour each, every week.

SECT. 20. Whenever any new teacher, except a master, is, in the opinion of the District Committee, needed for any school under their charge, said Committee shall, *before* making any appointment, examine the candidates in the manner required by law, and with special reference to the place which is then to be filled; and also as to their competency to teach the elements of articulation, of music and drawing; and in regard to teachers in the Grammar Schools, they shall consult with the master in whose school such teacher is to be appointed.* And the same course shall be pursued in all cases where it is proposed to transfer or to advance a teacher from one grade of school to another. Teachers so appointed shall be nominated by the District Committees, to this Board, for confirmation, and they shall be considered entitled to the established salary from the time of their entering upon their duties. It shall be the duty of the Secretary to give immediate information of such appointment to the City Auditor. Reappointed incumbents in the service of this Board shall rank as new teachers, and begin with the salary of such teachers.

SECT. 21. When, at any examination for assistant teachers, a larger number of candidates are found qualified than is required to fill the existing vacancies, it

Marginal notes: Examination of teachers. Teachers advanced to another grade to be examined. Reappointed teachers to be considered as new teachers. Names of well-qualified candidates at examinations to be preserved.

* The School Committee, unless the town at its annual meeting determines that the duty may be performed by the Prudential Committee, shall select and contract with the teachers of the public schools; shall require full and satisfactory evidence of the good moral character of all instructors who may be employed; and shall ascertain, by personal examination, their qualifications for teaching and capacity for the government of schools. (Gen. Stat. Ch. 38, § 23.)

shall be the duty of the Secretary of the District Committee making the examination, to keep a record of the names of such well-qualified candidates as the said Committee may direct, and to deposit such record with the Superintendent of Public Schools. This record shall give the names and addresses of the said candidates, and such information in regard to their qualifications, whether for Grammar or Primary Schools, as the said Committee may direct. And any District Committee may elect Assistants for the Grammar Schools, or Primary School Teachers, from the candidates so recommended, with or without a new examination, at the option of said Committee.

Canvassing the lists of teachers.

SECT. 22. In the month of May, annually, the Committee on the Latin School, the English High School, the Girls' High and Normal School, and each District Committee, in a meeting regularly called, shall canvass the list of teachers in their District, and, after consultation with the master, they shall decide upon the

Nomination of teachers for re-election.

persons whom they will recommend for re-election, and said Committee shall, at the annual meeting in June for the election of teachers, nominate the persons thus approved, who shall be considered the regular candidates for their respective offices. And in case any Committee have decided not to nominate any teacher for re-election, they may, if a majority of said Committee deem it expedient, give notice of their intention, to said teacher, before the annual election.

District Committees shall give advice to instructors, &c.

SECT. 23. The District Committee shall give their advice to the instructors in any emergency; and take cognizance of any difficulty which may have occurred between the instructors and parents of pupils, or between the instructors themselves, relative to the government or instruction of their schools. An appeal, however, to the whole Board, is not hereby denied to any citizen or instructor. In addition to the specific duties of the District Committees, it shall be their duty, generally, to make any temporary arrangement which they may find necessary for their schools, or for the convenience of the instructors, provided that nothing shall be done contrary to the School Regulations.

District Committees may make temporary arrangements.

SECT. 24. Each District Committee may transfer their own Primary School Teachers from one Primary School to another, and may change the location of their Primary Schools from one schoolroom to another, as they may think proper; but notice of any such transfer or change, and of the appointment of any new Primary School Teacher, shall, within one week after they are made, be sent to the Secretary of the Board, and the same shall be mentioned in the next quarterly report of the District Committee; and any teacher, of any grade, actually in the employ of the city, may be transferred by this Board, without re-examination, to any vacant place of the same grade in the city.

Transfer of Primary Schools and teachers.

Notice to be sent to Secretary of the Board.

Transfer of Teachers by the Board.

SECT. 25. The Committees on the Latin School, the English High School, the Girls' High and Normal School, and each District Committee, shall, during the month of July, make a thorough examination of their respective schools, and shall report at the quarterly meeting in September, the results of their examinations, together with such suggestions for the improvement of the schools as they may see fit to offer, and the statistics of each school in a tabular form, on the following points, viz: 1. The number of teachers; 2. The changes of teachers made during the year; 3. The number of different scholars registered; 4. The number of these received from other Public Schools of the city; 5. The number discharged; 6. The largest number present at

Annual examinations.

any one time ; 7. The largest average attendance for any one month, and the name of the month ; 8. The average attendance for the year ; 9. The number and names of the medal scholars, and the recipients of the Lawrence prizes ; 10. The number and ages of the candidates offered and admitted at the High Schools, from each of the Grammar Schools. These reports shall be referred to a Special Committee of the Board, who shall make from them such selections as they may think important for public information, and shall add thereto such suggestions and remarks as they shall deem expedient ; and their report, which shall be presented at the quarterly meeting in December, when accepted by the Board, shall be printed for distribution among the citizens.

Annual reports.

CHAPTER V.

Election of Instructors of Public Schools.

School year.   SECTION 1. The school year shall commence on the first Monday in September, and end on the day immediately preceding the first Monday in September.

Annual election of teachers.   SECT. 2. In the month of June, annually, the Board shall elect the instructors of the Public Schools, and fix their salaries* for the ensuing year. Said instructors

---

* The salaries of the Instructors in the various schools have been established as follows, for the present school year, viz : —

The salary of the Masters of the Latin, the English High, and the Girls' High and Normal Schools, is $ 2,600 for the first year's service, with an increase of $ 100 for each additional year's service till the salary amounts to $ 3,000 per annum.

The salary of the Sub-Masters of the Latin and English High Schools, and of the Masters of the Grammar Schools is $ 1,800 for the first year, with an annual increase of $ 100 till it amounts to $ 2,200.

shall rank as follows : 1st, Masters ; 2d, Sub-Masters ;
3d, Ushers ; 4th, Head Assistants ; 5th, Assistants ;
6th, Primary School Teachers ; 7th, Music Teachers ;
8th, Sewing Teachers.

Sᴇᴄᴛ. 3. The Masters of the several schools having Mode of choos-
been duly nominated by their respective District Com- ing instructors.

The salary of the Ushers of the Latin and English High Schools, and of the
Sub-Masters of the Grammar Schools, is $ 1,400 for the first year, with an
annual increase of $ 100 till it amounts to $ 1,800.

The salary of the Ushers of the Grammar Schools is $ 1,000 for the first year,
with an annual increase of $ 100, till it amounts to $ 1,200.

The salary of the Head Assistant of the Girls' High and Normal School is
$ 700 per annum, and the salary of the other Assistants in this School is $ 600
per annum.

The salary of the Teacher of the Normal Department of the Girls' High and
Normal School is $ 800 per annum.

The salary of the Head Assistants in the Grammar Schools is $ 600 per
annum ; and the salary of the other Assistants in the Grammar Schools, and of
the Teachers of the Primary Schools, is $ 400 for the first year, with an annual
increase of $ 50 till it amounts to $ 550 per annum.

The salary of the Music Teachers in the Grammar Schools is $ 125 per annum
for each school.

The salary of the Instructor in Vocal and Physical Gymnastics in the Grammar Schools is $ 1,500 per annum.

The salary of the Teacher of Music in the Primary Schools is $ 1,200 per
annum.

The salaries of the Sewing Teachers are as follows, — and the teachers shall
severally devote to instructing their pupils the time designated herein : —

The Sewing Teachers of the Adams, Lyman, and Wells Schools shall teach
sewing ten hours each week, and shall severally receive $ 225 per annum.

The Sewing Teachers of the Franklin, Lawrence, Lincoln, Bigelow, and Chap-
man Schools shall teach sewing twelve hours each week, and shall severally
receive $ 260 per annum.

The Sewing Teachers of the Hancock and Everett Schools shall teach sewing
sixteen hours each week, and shall each receive $ 300 per annum.

The Sewing Teacher of the Winthrop School shall teach sewing twenty hours
each week, and shall each receive $ 400 per annum.

The Sewing Teacher of the Bowditch School shall teach sewing twenty-
three hours each week, and shall receive $ 450 per annum.

The Salary of the Teacher of French in the Latin School is $ 500 per annum.
The salary of the Teacher of French in the Girls' High and Normal School is
$ 500 per annum. The salary of the Teacher of German in the Girls' High and
Normal School is $ 500 per annum. The salary of the Teacher of Drawing in
the Girls' High and Normal School is $ 900 per annum. The salary of the
Teacher of Drawing in the English High School is $ 500 per annum. The sal-
ary of the Teacher of Vocal Music in the Girls' High and Normal School is
$ 450 per annum.

mittees, shall be elected by ballot, and thirty votes at
least shall in all cases be necessary to a choice, and the
other instructors shall be elected by confirmation on
nomination of their respective Committees; but no teacher, except a Master, shall be elected by this Board,
without having served on trial at least three months in
the Boston schools.

Election of a
new master.

SECT. 4. Whenever a new Master is to be elected
for any of the Public Schools, the Secretary shall give
notice thereof in such newspapers, and for such length of
time, as the Board may direct, specifying in such notice
that all applications for the office must be made in writing,
and lodged with the Secretary, together with any written
evidence of qualifications which the candidate may wish
to present, on or before a day named in such notice.

Same.

SECT. 5. In case the vacancy to be filled is in the
Latin School, the English High School, or the Girls'
High and Normal School, the Committees of those
schools shall together constitute a committee for the
examination of candidates. But in case of a vacancy
in any of the Grammar Schools, the Examining Committee shall be composed of the District Committee of
the school in which the vacancy exists, and of the members for the two wards numerically nearest to the ward
in which said school is situated; and one third of the
members of either of these committees shall constitute a
quorum for doing business.

Same.

SECT. 6. The Examining Committee shall take from
the Secretary's files all the applications and written evidence, and shall have personal interviews with the applicants, and make inquiries as to their qualifications, and,
at a meeting appointed for the purpose, shall carefully
examine the candidates in the manner required by law,*

* See page 19 of these Rules.

and always with reference to the office that is then to be
filled. And none but said Committee, the members of
this Board, the Superintendent of Public Schools, and
the candidates under examination, shall be present.

SECT. 7. The Examining Committee shall report to *Examining Committee's* the Board, at some subsequent meeting, the names of *report.*
all the applicants who have been examined by them,
together with such other facts and circumstances respect-
ing the candidates, their recommendations and qualifications, as they may deem necessary for the information
of the Board. They shall also designate in their report
the names of two or more of the candidates whose examinations were most satisfactory, with the opinions of the
Examining Committee on their qualifications severally,
and the Board shall then proceed to a choice by ballot.

SECT. 8. The instructors elected at the annual meeting *Instructors to hold their offices for one year.* shall hold their offices for one school year, unless sooner
removed by vote of the Board.

CHAPTER VI.

Duties of the Secretary.

SECTION 1. The Secretary shall have charge of the *Records and files.* Records of the Board, and of all papers directed by
the Board to be kept on its files; he shall keep a per-
manent record-book, in which all its votes, orders, and
proceedings shall by him be recorded.

SECT. 2. He shall notify all stated and special meet- *Notices to be given.* ings; he shall notify the Chairman of every Committee
appointed, stating the commission, and the names of the
members associated with him; he shall notify the meetings of all Sub-Committees, when requested by the
Chairman or by any two members thereof; he shall

D

notify the instructors of their appointments, and shall give such other notices as the Board may require.

Report to Secretary of State.

SECT. 3. He shall prepare the Annual Report required by the statute of the Commonwealth, and he shall transmit the same, legally signed, to the Secretary of State, on or before the thirtieth day of April.*

Votes to be transmitted.

SECT. 4. He shall transmit copies of all votes, resolutions, and documents which are to be sent to the members of the Board, to the various Committees, to the Teachers, or to other persons.

Medals to be provided.

SECT. 5. He shall see that the Medals and Diplomas awarded to the successful candidates in the Public Schools are procured, properly inscribed, and sent to the appropriate schools at least one day preceding the Annual Exhibitions.

Examination of bills.

SECT. 6. He shalle xamine all bills for salaries, and the bills for all articles purchased by order of the Board, or by the Committee on Accounts, and shall perform such other duties as the School Committee shall prescribe, or from time to time direct.

CHAPTER VII.

Duties of the Superintendent.

Election.

SECTION 1. The Superintendent of Public Schools shall be elected annually, by ballot, at the quarterly meeting of the Board in June, to enter upon the duties of his office on the first day of September next ensuing.

Salary.

At the same meeting the salary of the Superintendent shall be voted, and no alteration in the amount of said salary shall be made during the year for which he is elected.

* See General Statutes, chapter 40.

Sect. 2. He shall devote himself to the study of the General duties. Public School System, and keep himself acquainted with the progress of instruction and discipline in other places, in order to suggest appropriate means for the advancement of the Public Schools in this city, and see that the regulations of the Board in regard to these schools are carried into full effect.

Sect. 3. He shall visit each school as often as his Visiting schools. other duties will permit, that he may obtain, as far as practicable, a personal knowledge of the condition of all the schools and be able to suggest improvements and remedy defects in their management. Shall advise the teachers on the best methods of instruction and discipline, and, to illustrate these methods in respect to Primary Schools, he shall hold occasional meetings of the teachers of the Meetings of Primary School schools, and have authority, for this purpose, to dismiss teachers. the Primary Schools at such times as he shall deem advisable, not exceeding one half day in each quarter. He has authority, also, to dismiss the Grammar Schools, not ex- Meetings of Grammar ceeding one half day in each half year, for the purpose of School teachers. holding meetings of the teachers of these schools.

Sect. 4. Whenever vacancies occur in the State State scholarscholarships to which this city is entitled, it shall be his ships. duty to give public notice thereof, and he shall be authorized, in conjunction with the chairman of each of the High School Committees, to examine candidates for said vacancies, and report to this Board the names of those to be recommended, according to law,* to the Board of Education. He shall make investigations as to the number and the condition of the children of the city who are not receiving the benefits offered by the Absentees from school. Public Schools, and shall endeavor to ascertain the reasons, and to suggest and apply the remedies.

* Gen. Stat. chap. 37, § 3.

Assistance to committees.

SECT. 5.   He shall render such aid and communicate such information to the various Committees as they may require of him, and shall assist them, when desired, in the quarterly examinations.   He shall see that all school registers, books of records, circulars, blanks for monthly reports of teachers, and annual reports of District Committees are prepared after uniform patterns, and ready to be furnished when needed.

Building and altering of Schoolhouses.

SECT. 6.   He shall consult with the different bodies who have control of the building and altering of schoolhouses, and shall communicate to them such information on the subject as he may possess; and he shall suggest such plans for building and altering schoolhouses as he

School expenses.

may consider best for the health and convenience of the teachers and pupils, and most economical for the city; and he shall advise with those through whom, either directly or indirectly, the school appropriations are expended, that there may result more uniformity in their plans and more economy in their expenditures.

SECT. 7.   It shall be his duty to attend the meetings of the Board, except when the subject of his own election is under consideration, and, when called upon through the President, to express his opinion on any subject under discussion, or to communicate such information as may be in his power.   At the quarterly meet-

Attend meetings of Board.

ings in March and September, he shall present to the Board a semi-annual Report, in print, giving an account of the schools he has visited, and of the other duties he has performed, together with such facts and suggestions relating to the condition of the schools, and the increase of their efficiency and usefulness, as he may deem advis-

Semi-annual report.

able.   He shall also embrace in his report an abstract of the semi-annual returns of the Public Schools, and a schedule showing the number of teachers then employed

in the schools; and these reports shall be referred to the
Special Committee on the Annual Report of the School
Board.

Sect. 8.   He shall keep a record of the names, ages, *Record of names of appli-* and residences of persons who may desire to be consid- *cants.* ered as candidates for the office of Assistant or Primary
School Teacher, with such remarks and suggestions re-
specting them as he may deem important for the information of Committees; which record shall be at all
times open to the inspection of any member of this
Board.   And he shall perform such other duties as the
School Committee shall prescribe, or from time to time
direct.

— —

CHAPTER VIII.

General Regulations of the Public Schools.

Section 1.   All teachers in the Public Schools are *Teachers to ob- serve the school* required to make themselves familiar with these Regula- *regulations.* tions, and especially with the portion that relates to their
own duties, and to the instruction and discipline of their
respective schools, and to see that these are faithfully
observed.

Sect. 2.   The instructors shall punctually observe *General duties of teachers.* the hours appointed for opening and dismissing the
schools; and, during school hours, shall faithfully de-
vote themselves to the public service.   In all their inter-
course with their scholars they shall strive to impress on
their minds, both by precept and example, the great
importance of continued efforts for improvement in morals, in manners and deportment, as well as in useful
learning.

School hours. Sect. 3. From the first Monday in May to the first Monday in September, the Grammar and Primary Schools shall commence their morning sessions at 8 o'clock, and close at 11 o'clock; and shall begin their afternoon sessions at 2 o'clock, and close at 5 o'clock. From the first Monday in September to the first Monday in May, they shall commence their morning sessions at 9 o'clock, and close at 12 o'clock; and shall begin their afternoon sessions at 2 o'clock, and shall close at 5 o'clock, except that from the third Monday in October to the first Monday in March, they may omit the afternoon recess and close at 4 o'clock. *Provided,* that nothing in this section shall be so construed as to prevent the teacher from the judicious exercise of the right to detain a pupil for a reasonable time after the regular hour for dismissing school, either for purposes of discipline, or to make up neglected lessons.

Teachers and pupils to be at school early. Sect. 4. All the schoolrooms shall be opened, and the teachers be present, both morning and afternoon, *fifteen minutes* before the time fixed for the session to begin. The teachers shall require the scholars to be in their seats, and shall commence and close the exercises of the schools, punctually at the prescribed hours.

Opening the schools. Sect. 5. The morning exercises of all the schools shall commence with the reading of a portion of the Scriptures, by the teacher, in each school; the reading to be followed by the Lord's Prayer, repeated by the teacher alone. The afternoon session shall close with appropriate singing.

Moral instruction. Sect. 6. Good morals being of the first importance to the pupils, and essential to their highest progress in useful knowledge, instruction therein shall be daily given in each of the schools.* The pupils shall be carefully

---

* "It shall be the duty of the president, professors, and tutors of the University at Cambridge, and of the several colleges, and of all preceptors and

instructed to avoid idleness and profanity, falsehood and deceit, and every wicked and disgraceful practice, and to conduct themselves in an orderly and proper manner; and it shall be the duty of the instructors, so far as practicable, to exercise a general inspection over them in these regards, both in and out of school, and also while going to the same and returning home; and on all suitable occasions to inculcate upon them the principles of truth and virtue.

SECT. 7. The principal teacher in every school shall keep a register in which shall be recorded the names, ages, dates of admission, and places of residence of the scholars. In addition to this register, other records shall be kept, in which shall be entered the daily absence of the scholars, and such notes of their class-exercises as may exhibit a view of their advancement and standing. *School register and records.*

SECT. 8. All school registers and other books for records, as well as all blanks for monthly reports, and circulars required in the several schools, shall be after uniform patterns, to be determined by the Superintendent of Public Schools, to whom all teachers are expected to apply whenever such articles are needed by them. *Blanks for schools.*

SECT. 9. Each master shall make a careful examination of his school as often as he can consistently with *Masters to examine their schools.*

teachers of academies, and all other instructors of youth, to exert their best endeavors to impress on the minds of children and youth committed to their care and instruction, the principles of piety, justice, and a sacred regard to truth, love to their country, humanity and universal benevolence, sobriety, industry and frugality, chastity, moderation, and temperance, and those other virtues which are the ornament of human society, and the basis upon which a republican constitution is founded; and it shall be the duty of such instructors to endeavor to lead their pupils, as their ages and capacities will admit, into a clear understanding of the tendency of the above-mentioned virtues to preserve and perfect a republican constitution, and secure the blessings of liberty, as well as to promote their future happiness and also to point out to them the evil tendency of the opposite vices." [Gen. Stat. chap. 38, § 10.]

proper attention to the pupils under his immediate charge.

SECT. 10. During the week preceding the quarterly meeting in March and in September, the principal teacher in each school shall make to the Superintendent of Public Schools semi-annual returns of the number of pupils belonging to the school, conformably to the blanks furnished for this purpose. They shall also include in their reports the names of those pupils belonging to their respective schools whose parents or guardians do not reside in the city, with the dates of their respective admissions.

Notices to be given to the Secretary.

SECT. 11. Each master shall, within one week after the appointment of a teacher, send to the secretary of this Board the full name of such teacher, with the precise date of his or her commencing service in his school; and if the person appointed has previously been in the service of the city as a teacher, he shall state where, when, and how long, such service was rendered. In like manner he shall give notice when any teacher shall have relinquished service in his school.

Teachers visiting schools.

SECT. 12. The instructors may, for the purpose of observing the modes of discipline, and instruction, visit any of the Public Schools in the city; but such visits shall not be made oftener than once a quarter, nor till provisions satisfactory to the Chairman of the District Committee or of the Sub-Committee has been made for the proper care of the pupils under their immediate charge.

Corporal punishment.

SECT. 13. All instructors shall aim at such discipline in their schools as would be exercised by a kind, judicious parent in his family; shall avoid corporal punishment in all cases where good order can be preserved by milder measures; and in no case shall resort be had to confinement in a closet or wardrobe, or to other cruel or unusual punishment, as a mode of discipline. It shall be the duty of the several masters and teachers in the public schools, at the close of each month, to make, in writing, to the Chairmen of their District Committees, a report of all cases in which corporal punishment has been inflicted; which report shall state the name of the pupil, the amount of punishment, and the reason for its infliction; and the Chairman of each District Committee shall, in his quarterly report, give the number of cases of corporal punishment during the previous quarter, and the average to each teacher of the District. Corporal punishment shall be inflicted only after the nature of the offence has been fully explained to the scholar, and shall be restricted to blows on the hand with a rattan, except in cases where a pupil refuses to submit to such punishment. Corporal punishment shall not be inflicted on a girl in a grammar school without the consent and approval of the master, which, in each individual case, must first be obtained.

SECT. 14. For violent or pointed opposition to authority in any particular instance, a principal teacher may exclude a child from school for the time being; and thereupon shall inform the parent or guardian of the measure, and shall apply to the District Committee for advice and direction. Whenever any scholar is absent from school, the teacher shall immediately ascertain the reason; and, if such absence be not occasioned by sickness or other sufficient cause, or is not satisfactorily explained, such pupil, with the consent of the Sub-Committee, may be suspended or discharged from the school, and a record of such proceeding shall be made. *Exclusion of a pupil.*

SECT. 15. When the example of any pupil in school is very injurious, and in all cases where reformation *Suspension and restoration of pupils.*

E

appears hopeless, it shall be the duty of the principal teacher, with the approbation of the Committee on the schools, to suspend such pupil from the school. But any child under this public censure, who shall have expressed to the teacher his regret for his folly or indiscretion, as openly and explicitly as the nature of the case may require, and shall have given evidence of amendment, shall, with the previous consent of said Committee, be reinstated in the privileges of the school.

SECT. 16. Whenever a teacher has satisfactory evidence that a pupil has left school without the intention of returning, such pupil's name shall forthwith be stricken from the list; but any absence recorded against the name of the pupil before the teacher receives this notice shall be allowed to remain, and be regarded the same as any other absences. When a pupil is absent from school more than five consecutive school days, the name of such pupil shall be stricken from the list at the end of the five days; and the absences shall in all cases be recorded while the name remains on the list. The name of a pupil who is suspended from school by any rules of the School Board, shall be stricken from the list, and any pupil shall be considered as absent whose attendance at school shall not continue for at least one half of the regular school session of the half day. In noting the absences of pupils, the short vacations shall be disregarded, and pupils who are not present on the first half day of a term after either of those vacations, shall be marked as absent.

Instructors, in cases of difficulty, to apply to District Committees.

SECT. 17. In cases of difficulty in the discharge of their official duties, or when they may desire any temporary aid, the instructors shall apply to the District Committees of their respective schools for advice and assistance.

Sect. 18. Whenever any instructor shall be absent from school, and a temporary instructor rendered necessary, the amount required to pay said substitute shall be withdrawn from the salary of the absentee; unless upon a representation of the case, by petition, and a report on said petition from the Standing Committee on Salaries, the Board shall order an allowance to be made. And no substitute shall be employed in any of the Primary Schools for more than one day at a time, without the approbation of one or more of the Sub-Committee of the school; nor in any department of the Grammar Schools without the approbation of two or more of the District Committee, the Chairman being one of them. The compensation per day allowed for substitutes in the Primary Schools, and for Assistants in the Grammar Schools, shall be $1.25; for Assistants in the Girls' High and Normal School, $1.50; for Ushers in the Grammar Schools, $2.75; for Sub-Masters in those schools, and for Ushers in the Latin and English High Schools, $3.75; for Sub-Masters in the Latin and English High Schools, and for Masters in the Grammar Schools, $5.00; for Masters in the Latin, English High, and Girls' High and Normal Schools, $6.00; for each day, counting six school days in the week, during which such substitute shall be employed. The compensation of temporary teachers shall be the same as that of substitutes.

Absentees must pay their substitutes.

Sect. 19. It shall be the duty of all the instructors to give vigilant attention to the ventilation and temperature of their schoolrooms. A regular system of ventilation shall be practised, as well in winter as in summer, by which the air in the rooms shall be effectually changed at each recess, and at the end of each school session before the house shall be closed.

Temperature and ventilation.

Examination of cellars and unoccupied rooms in season of fires.

SECT. 20. The Masters of the Grammar Schools shall examine, or cause some competent person connected with each school to examine, during the season of fires, the cellars and unoccupied rooms in their respective buildings; such examinations to be made during the first and every succeeding hour of the forenoon and afternoon sessions, and the result made known to the master of the school.

Recesses.

SECT. 21. There shall be a recess of fifteen minutes for every pupil each half day, including the time occupied in going out and coming in, which shall take place as nearly as may be at the expiration of one half of each school session.

Physical exercise in schools.

SECT. 22. The masters, ushers, and teachers, in the Public Schools shall so arrange the daily course of exercise in their respective classes that every scholar shall have daily, in the forenoon and afternoon, some kind of physical or gymnastic exercise; this exercise to take place as nearly as practicable midway between the commencement of the session and recess, and between recess and the end of the session.

Care of school premises.

SECT. 23. The principal teachers of the several schools shall prescribe such rules for the use of the yards and out-buildings connected with the schoolhouses as shall insure their being kept in a neat and proper condition, and shall examine them as often as may be necessary for such purpose, and they shall be held responsible for any want of neatness or cleanliness on their premises; and when anything is out of order they must give immediate notice thereof to the Superintendent of Public Buildings.

Things not allowed.

SECT. 24. No instructor in the Public Schools shall be allowed to teach in any other public school than that to which he or she has been appointed, nor to keep a

private school of any description whatever, nor to attend
to the instruction of any private pupils before 6 o'clock,
P. M., except on Wednesday and Saturday afternoons,
nor to engage as editor of any newspaper, or of any
religious or political periodical.

SECT. 25. The instructors shall not award medals or Same.
other prizes to the pupils under their charge ; nor shall
instructors become the recipients during term-time, and Presents.
only from a graduating class at any other time, of any
present of money, or other property, from the pupils.
No subscription or contribution for any purpose what- Subscription or
ever, shall be introduced into any public school.   contribution.

SECT. 26. No person whatever shall read to the No advertise-
pupils of any school, or post upon the walls of any to the pupils.
school building, or fences of the same, any advertise-
ment. Nor shall any agent or other person be per- No agent to ex-
mitted to enter any school for the purpose of exhibiting, school.
either to teacher or pupils, any new book or article of
apparatus.:

SECT. 27. The books used and the studies pursued Authorized
in all the Public Schools shall be such, and such only, as studies.
may be authorized by the Board ; and the teachers shall
not permit any books, tracts, or other publications to be
distributed in their schools.

SECT. 28. No pupils shall be allowed to retain their Pupils must
connection with any of the Public Schools unless they and utensils
are furnished with the books and utensils regularly required.
required to be used in the respective classes.

SECT. 29. In cases where children are in danger of Books, &c., for
being deprived of the advantages of education, by reason dren.
of inability to obtain books, through the poverty or
negligence of parents or guardians, the Committee on
Accounts are authorized, on behalf of the School Committee, to carry out the provisions of the Statute on this

subject.* During the first week in April, annually, the principal teacher in each Grammar School, and the teacher of each Primary School, shall make to the Secretary of the Board, a return of the names of all scholars supplied with books at the expense of the city, the names of the books so furnished, together with the names of the parents, guardians, or masters of said pupils; and suitable blanks shall be provided for this purpose by the Secretary.

Children entitled to attend the public schools.

SECT. 30. All children living within the limits of the city, who are not otherwise disqualified, and who are upwards of five years of age, shall be entitled to attend the public schools of the city; but no child whose residence is not in the city, or who has only a temporary residence in it for the purpose of attending the Public Schools, shall be received or retained in any school, except upon the consent previously obtained of the District Committee; and said District Committee may, in accordance with the provisions of the General Statutes, require the parent or guardian of such child, to pay a sum equal to the average cost per scholar of such school, for such period as said child may attend thereat.†

*"If any scholar is not furnished by his parent, master, or guardian, with the requisite books, he shall be supplied therewith by the School Committee at the expense of the town.

"The School Committee shall give notice, in writing, to the assessors of the town, of the names of the scholars supplied with books under the provisions of the preceding section, of the books so furnished, the prices thereof, and the names of the parents, masters, or guardians, who ought to have supplied the same. The assessors shall add the price of the books to the next annual tax of such parents, masters, or guardians; and the amount so added shall be levied, collected, and paid into the town treasury, in the same manner as the town taxes.

"If the assessors are of opinion that any parent, master, or guardian, is unable to pay the whole expense of the books so supplied on his account, they shall omit to add the price of such books, or shall only add a part thereof to his annual tax, according to their opinion of his ability to pay." [Gen. Stat. chap. 38, §§ 30, 31, 32.]

†"All children within the Commonwealth may attend the public schools in

SECT. 31. No pupil shall be admitted to the priv- Same.
ilege of one school who has been expelled from another,
or while under suspension, unless by vote of the Board.

SECT. 32. No pupil shall be admitted into any of Certificate of vaccination.
the Public Schools without a certificate from a physician
that he or she has been vaccinated, or otherwise secured
against the smallpox; but this certificate shall not be
required of pupils who go from one public school to
another.

SECT. 33. No child who comes to school without Cleanliness of pupils required.
proper attention having been given to the *cleanliness* of
his person and of his dress, or whose clothes are not
properly repaired, shall be permitted to remain in school,
.but shall be sent home to be prepared for school in a
proper manner.

SECT. 34. Tardiness shall be subject to such penalty Tardiness and absence of pupils.
as in each case the teacher may think proper. No pupil
shall be allowed to be absent any part of the regular
school hours for the purpose of receiving instruction, or
taking lessons of any kind, elsewhere. Pupils detained Dismission of pupils before the close of the session.
at home must, on returning to school, bring an excuse
for such detention; and every pupil, wishing on any day
to be dismissed before the close of the session, must
assign satisfactory reasons therefor and obtain the consent
of the teacher. Teachers having charge of pupils who
are habitually truant shall report their names and resi- Truancy.

the place in which they have their legal residence, subject to the regulations
prescribed by law." [Gen. Stat. chap. 41, § 3.]
   " With the consent of school committees first obtained, children between the
ages of five and fifteen may attend schools in cities and towns other than those
in which their parents or guardians reside; but whenever a child resides in a
city or town different from that of the residence of the parent or guardian,
for the sole purpose of attending school there, the parent or guardian of such
child shall be liable to pay to such city or town, for tuition, a sum equal to the
average expense per scholar for such school, for the period the child shall have
so attended." [Gen. Stat. chap 41, § 7.]

dences, and the names of their parents or guardians, to the truant officers of the district.

Annual exhibitions.

Sect. 35. There shall be an annual exhibition of the Latin School on the Saturday, and of the English High School on the Monday, preceding the third Wednesday in July; and on the Tuesday following said Wednesday there shall be an exhibition of the several Grammar Schools; at which exhibitions the medals and diplomas shall be conferred upon the pupils. *Provided, however,* that the District Committees on the several Grammar Schools for *girls* may, if they deem it advisable, direct that such exhibition shall be on the Monday, instead of on the Tuesday, following said Wednesday. The hours for the exhibitions of the several schools shall be arranged by the President of the Board. The Exhibitions of the Grammar Schools shall be conducted in such manner as shall best present the actual condition of each school in the prominent branches of study, and shall not exceed two hours in length. On the first five school days of the week previous to the Exhibition, the parents and friends of the children shall be invited to witness the usual exercises of the school, and on the last day of that week the several Grammar Schools shall be closed. And in the afternoon of the day of the Annual Exhibitions of the

School festival. Grammar Schools, the Annual School Festival shall be held, to which members of the School Committee, all the teachers in the public Schools, and the medal scholars of the current year shall be invited.

Holidays and vacations.

Sect. 36. The following holidays and vacations shall be granted to the schools, viz: every Wednesday and Saturday afternoon, throughout the year; Christmas day, New Year's day, the Twenty-second of February, Good Friday, Fast day, May day, Artillery Election, and the Fourth of July; Thanksgiving week; the week imme-

diately preceding the first Monday in March ; one week
commencing on the Monday preceding the last Wednesday in May ; and the remainder of the school year following their respective exhibitions ; and to the Girls' High
and Normal School from the Monday following the third
Wednesday in July to the Saturday next preceding the
second Monday in September. The Primary Schools
shall be allowed the holidays and vacations of the Grammar Schools, and also the day preceding and the day of
the annual Exhibition of the Grammar Schools ; and the
President of the Board is authorized to suspend the
schools *on such public occasions* as he may think proper,
not exceeding three days in any one municipal year.
In addition to these holidays the Latin and English
High Schools shall be entitled to the two days of public
exhibition at Harvard University. No other holidays
shall be allowed except by special vote of the Board ;
and no school shall be suspended on any other occasion,
except for special and important reasons relating to a
particular school, and then only by express permission
of the Sub-Committee.

SECT. 37. On the 21st of February, annually, the
Masters of the High and Grammar School shall assem-
ble their pupils, each in the hall of his schoolhouse,
and read to them, or cause to be read to them, by one
or more of their own number, extracts from Washington's
Farewell Address to the People of the United States,
combining therewith other patriotic exercises ; and the
regular exercises of the session shall be suspended so far
as is necessary to give opportunity to this reading.

Reading of Washington's Farewell Address.

F

CHAPTER IX.

Regulations of the Primary Schools.

Admission of pupils to Primary Schools.

SECTION 1.   Every teacher shall admit to her school all applicants of suitable age and qualifications, residing nearest to the school under her charge, provided the number in her school will warrant the admission ; and in all cases of doubt or difficulty in the discharge of this duty, she shall apply to her Sub-Committee for advice and direction.

Transfer of pupils.

SECT. 2.   When any child shall apply to be admitted from another Primary School, the teacher shall require a certificate of transfer from the teacher of the former school ; which certificate shall serve instead of a Certificate of Vaccination.

Promotion to Grammar Schools.

SECT. 3.   The regular promotion of scholars to the Grammar Schools shall be made semi-annually, on the first Monday in March, and on the first Monday in September.   But occasionally promotions may be made on Monday of any week, whenever the Sub-Committee of the Primary School and the Master of the Grammar School may deem it *necessary.*

Schools for special instruction.

SECT. 4.   One or more schools for the special instruction of children *over seven years of age,* and not qualified for the Grammar School, may be established in each District.   The course of study shall be the same as in the Primary Schools ; and it shall be in the power of each District Committee to introduce Writing, and the elements of Written Arithmetic.   Any scholar over eight years of age, and not in the first or second class, may be removed from any Primary School to a school for special instruction, at the discretion of the Sub-Committee.

Sect. 5. *The School on the Western Avenue shall be* connected with the Phillips School District. Children over eight years of age may be admitted into this school at the discretion of the Sub-Committee; and their studies shall conform to the regulations of the Grammar Schools.

School on Western Avenue.

Sect. 6. The teachers shall attend to the physical education and comfort of the pupils under their care. When, from the state of the weather or other causes, the recesses in the open air shall be impracticable, the children may be exercised within the room, in accordance with the best judgment and ability of the teachers. In the schools which are kept in buildings occupied by Grammar Schools, the recesses shall be arranged by the masters so as not to interfere with the exercises of those schools.

Proper care of the pupils in school.

Recesses for Primary schools in Grammar school buildings.

Sect. 7. The schools shall contain, as nearly as practicable, an equal number of pupils, the maximum number being fifty-six; and the pupils in each of the schools shall be arranged in six classes, unless otherwise ordered by the District Committee.

Number of pupils to a school.

Classes.

Sect. 8. Plain sewing may be introduced into any Primary School, at the discretion of the Sub-Committee, and singing shall form part of the opening and closing exercises of every session; and such time be devoted to instruction in Music in each school as the Sub-Committee may deem expedient.

Sewing.

Singing.

Sect. 9. *The following Books and Studies shall be attended to in the respective classes. The* ORDER *of the exercises and lessons assigned to each class to be determined by the teacher; subject, however, to the direction of the Committee of the school.*

SIXTH CLASS.

Hillard's First Primary Reader to the 30th page ; the words in columns to be spelled without book, and also words selected from the reading lessons.

Boston Primary School Tablets. Number Eleven, — the words and elementary sounds repeated after the teacher. Number One, — the name and sound of each letter, including the long and short sound of each vowel. Number Fifteen to be read and spelled by letters and by sound, and read by calling the words at sight. Number Sixteen to be read by spelling, and by calling words at sight, with oral lessons on the meaning of the sentences. Number Thirteen to be spelled by sounds. Numbers Nine and Ten to. be used in reviewing the alphabet, for variety of forms of letters. Number Five, — the pupil to name and point out the lines and plane figures. Number Two, — analyze the forms of the capitals, and tell what lines compose each.

Boston Primary School Slate, No. 1. — Print the small letters, and draw the straight lines and the rectilinear figures. The blackboard and tablets to be used in teaching the slate exercises.

Develop the idea of numbers to ten, by the use of objects. Count to one hundred on the numeral frame.

Repeating verses and maxims. Oral lessons on size, form, and color, illustrated by objects in the school-room ; also upon common plants, and animals, illustrated by the objects themselves or by pictures.

Learning to read and spell from letter and word cards, at the option of the teacher.

Singing for five or ten minutes twice at least each day.

Physical exercises for five or ten minutes, twice at least each session.

FIFTH CLASS.

Hillard's First Primary Reader, as in the sixth class, completed.

My First School Book, for spelling to the 24th page, and for reading to the 70th page.

Boston Primary School Tablets. Review the exercises on Tablets prescribed for the sixth Class. Number Nineteen, entire, and Number Twenty to L. Number Six, — name and point out the figures, and their parts. Number Eleven to be taught from the tablet. Number Fourteen, — syllables to be spelled by sound.

Boston Primary School Slate, No. 1. Review the slate exercises prescribed for the Sixth Class. Print the capital letters, also short words; draw the curvilinear figures.

Counting real objects, and counting with the numeral frame by twos to one hundred.

Repeating verses and maxims. Oral lessons on form, size, and color, and on plants, and animals. Singing and physical exercises as above.

FOURTH CLASS.

My First School Book, completed both as a reader and a speller.

Hillard's Second Primary Reader, to the 50th page; the words in columns to be spelled, and also words selected from the reading lessons. Spelling words by sounds.

Boston Primary School Tablets. Numbers Five and Six reviewed, with description or analysis of the lines and figures. Numbers Eleven, Thirteen, and Fourteen, reviewed. Numbers Twelve and Twenty to be learned. Numbers Seventeen and Eighteen, — names of punctuation marks.

Boston Primary School Slate, No. 1, — used daily. Copies in printing and drawing reviewed and completed. Printing four or five words daily. Writing Arabic figures.

Adding and subtracting numbers to twenty, illustrated by objects and the numeral frame. Counting on the numeral frame by twos to one hundred, and by threes to fifty.

Repeating verses and maxims. Oral lessons on objects as above, with their parts, qualities, and uses. Singing and physical exercises as above.

THIRD CLASS.

Hillard's Second Primary Reader, completed; the words in columns to be spelled, and also words selected from the reading lessons. At each lesson in reading and spelling, words spelled by sounds. Conversations on the meaning of what is read.

Spelling and Thinking Combined, — to the thirty-fifth page. Spelling. words by sounds. Questions on the meaning of words.

• *Boston Primary School Tablets.* Numbers Five, Six, Eleven, Twelve, Thirteen, Fourteen, and Twenty, reviewed. Number Three. Number Eighteen, — use of punctuation marks commenced.

Boston Primary School Slate, No. 2. Write the small script letters and draw the plane figures. Exercises in writing and drawing to be illustrated by tablets and blackboard. Print a few words in capitals.

Eaton's Primary School Arithmetic begun. Miscellaneous questions in adding and subtracting small numbers. Practical questions involving similar combinations. The idea of multiplication devolving by the use of the numeral frame. Numbers to be combined, occasionally written on slates from dictation.

Repeating verses and maxims. Abbreviations. Oral lessons as above, and upon common objects, and the senses. Singing and physical exercises as above.

SECOND CLASS.

Hillard's Third Primary Reader, to the 100th page; the words in columns to be spelled, and also words selected from the reading lessons. Difficult words to be spelled by sounds. Conversations on the meaning of what is read.

Spelling and Thinking Combined, — to the seventy-fifth page. Spelling words by sounds. Questions on the meaning of words.

Eaton's Primary Arithmetic, — addition, subtraction, and multiplication tables to be learned, and the practical questions under these rules to be attended to.

Boston Primary School Tablets. Numbers Three, Five, Six, Eleven, Twelve, and Eighteen, to be reviewed. Number Seven, — drawing and oral lessons on the objects represented. Number eighteen, — uses and definitions of points and marks learned, and applied in reading lessons.

Boston Primary School Slate, No. 2. Writing capital and small letters, and drawing planes and solids, with illustrations from tablets and blackboard. Writing short words. Review abbreviations and Roman numerals.

Repeating verses and maxims. Oral lessons on objects, trades, and the most common phenomena of nature. Singing and physical exercises as above.

FIRST CLASS.

Hillard's Third Primary Reader, completed; with definitions, explanations, spelling, by letters and by sounds; also questions on punctuation, the use of capitals, and the marks indicating the pronunciation.

Spelling and Thinking Combined, completed. Spelling words by sounds. Questions on the meaning of words.

Eaton's Primary Arithmetic, completed. The tables of multiplication and division to 12+12 and 144÷12. Notation to 1,000. Counting by threes and fours, forwards to a hundred, and backwards, from a hundred to one. Practical questions to be attended to.

Boston Primary School Tablets. Review those used in the Second Class. Frequent drill on Number Twelve. Number eight, drawing and oral lessons on the objects represented.

Boston Primary School Slate, No. 2. Writing capitals and small letters, the pupil's name, and words from the spelling lessons, with particular care to imitate the letters on the frame. Drawing all the copies on the frame.

Repeating verses and maxims. Review abbreviations. Oral lessons on objects, trades, occupations, with exercise of observation by noting the properties and qualities of objects, comparing and classifying them, considering their uses, the countries from which they come, and their modes of production, preparation, or fabrication.

Singing and physical exercises as above.

SECT. 10. No scholars are to be promoted from one class to another till they are familiar with all the lessons of the class from which they are to be transferred, except for special reasons, satisfactory to the Sub-Committee.

CHAPTER X.

Regulations of Grammar Schools.

Second grade. SECTION 1. These schools form the second grade in the system of public instruction established in this city.

The following are their names, locations, and dates of establishment : —

Name.	Location.	Sex.	Total lishe t.
1 — Eliot School	North Bennet Street	For Boys	1713
2 — Franklin School	Ringgold Street	" Girls	1785
3 — Mayhew School	Hawkins Street	" Boys	1803
4 — Boylston School	Fort Hill	" Boys	1819
5 — Bowdoin School	Myrtle Street	" Girls	1821
6 — Hancock School	Richmond Place	" Girls	1822
7 — Wells School	Blossom Street	" Girls	1833
8 — Winthrop School	Tremont Street	" Girls	1836
9 — Lyman School	East Boston	" Boys and Girls	1837
10 — Lawrence School	South Boston	" Boys and Girls	1844
11 — Brimmer School	Common Street	" Boys	1844
12 — Phillips School	Southac Street	" Boys	1844
13 — Dwight School	Springfield Street	" Boys	1844
14 — Quincy School	Tyler Street	" Boys	1847
15 — Bigelow School	South Boston	" Boys and Girls	1849
16 — Chapman School	East Boston	" Boys and Girls	1849
17 — Adams School	East Boston	" Boys and Girls	1850
18 — Lincoln School	South Boston	" Boys and Girls	1859
19 — Everett School	Northampton Street	" Girls	1860
20 — Bowditch School	South Street	" Girls	1861

In these schools are taught the common branches of an English Education.

SECT. 2. The schools for boys shall each be instructed by a master, a sub-master, an usher, a head assistant, and three or more female assistants. *Instructors in boys' schools.*

The schools for girls shall each be instructed by a master, a head-assistant for each story in the building, and three or more female assistants. *In girls' schools.*

The mixed schools (boys' and girls') shall each be instructed by a master, a sub-master, a head assistant for each story in the building, and three or more female assistants. *In mixed schools.*

Any existing exceptions to the foregoing organizations, authorized by special vote of the Board, shall remain until otherwise ordered.

SECT. 3. Each school shall be allowed a teacher for every fifty-six pupils on the register, and an additional female assistant may be appointed whenever there are *Number of pupils to a teacher.*

thirty scholars above the employment for the teachers
already in the school, if the District Committee deem it
expedient; and whenever the number of pupils on the
register shall be reduced to thirty less than such comple-
ment, one female assistant may be removed from such
school, if the District Committee recommend it; *provided*, that, in determining the number of teachers to
which any school may be entitled under this section, one
head assistant shall not be counted.

Qualifications
for admission
to the Gram-
mar Schools.

SECT. 4. Any pupil may be admitted into the Grammar Schools who, on examination by the master or any
of his assistants, shall be found able to read, at first
sight, easy prose; to spell common words of one, two,
or three syllables; to distinguish and name the marks of
punctuation; to perform mentally such simple questions
in Addition, Subtraction, and Division, as are found in
Eaton's Primary Arithmetic; to answer readily to any
proposed combination of the Multiplication Table in
which neither factor exceeds ten; to read and write
Arabic numbers containing three figures, and the Roman
numerals as far as the sign of one hundred; and to
enunciate, clearly and accurately, the elementary sounds
of our language. And no pupil who does not possess
these qualifications shall be admitted into any Grammar
School, except by special permit of the District Committee.

Examination of
primary schol-
ars for promo-
tion to Gram-
mar School.

Certificates of
admission.

SECT. 5. Within the two weeks preceding the first
Monday in March, annually, the Master of each Grammar School shall visit each Primary which is expected
to send pupils to his schools; and he shall examine the
first class in each of said schools, and shall give certificates of admission to the Grammar School to such as he
may find qualified in accordance with the foregoing re-
quirements. But in the month of July, annually, each

teacher in the Primary Schools shall accompany her first class to such Grammar Schoolhouse in the vicinity as the master may designate, when he and his assistants shall examine the candidates for admission to the Grammar School, in presence of their instructors, and shall give certificates to those who are found to be properly qualified. If, however, the parent or guardian of any applicant not admitted on the examination of the master, is dissatisfied with his decision, such person may appeal to the District Committee for another examination of said applicant.

SECT. 6. Pupils admitted from the Primary Schools are expected to enter the Grammar Schools on the first Monday of March and of September; but all other applicants residing in the District, found on examination *qualified in all respects*, may enter the Grammar Schools by applying to the master at the schoolhouse, on Monday morning of any week when the schools are in session. Pupils regularly transferred from one Grammar School to another, may be admitted at any time, on presenting their certificates of transfer, without an examination.

Times of admitting pupils to Grammar Schools.

SECT. 7. No lessons shall be assigned to girls to be studied out of school; and, in assigning out-of-school lessons to boys, the instructors shall not assign a longer lesson daily than a boy of good capacity can acquire by an hour's study; nor shall the lessons to be studied in school be so long as to require a scholar of ordinary capacity to study out of school in order to learn them; and no out-of-school lessons shall be assigned on Saturday.

Out-of-school lessons.

SECT. 8. Each school or department of a school shall be divided into four classes. Each class shall consist of two or more divisions, each of which sections shall pursue the studies and use the text-books assigned to

Classes and sections.

its class; but whenever it shall appear that a division of
a lower class has, in any particular branch of study, made
the attainments requisite for promotion to a higher class,
at a period earlier than the regular time for general promotion, then such division may, at the discretion of the
master, and with the approval of the Committee, enter
upon the study of one of the text-books prescribed for
the next higher class.

Text-books.   SECT. 9. The books and exercises of the several
classes shall be as follows, viz : —

Same.   *Class* 4. — No. 1. Worcester's Spelling Book. 2.
Hillard's Fourth Reader. 3. Writing in each school,
in such Writing Books as the District Committee may
approve.   4. Drawing in Bartholomew's Drawing
Books. 5. Eaton's Intellectual Arithmetic, with lessons in Written Arithmetic on the slate and blackboard. 6. Warren's Primary Geography.

Same.   *Class* 3. — No. 1. Worcester's Spelling Book. 2.
Hillard's Intermediate Reader. 3. Writing, as in
Fourth Class. 4. Eaton's Intellectual Arithmetic, and
Eaton's Common School Arithmetic, revised edition.
5. Drawing in Bartholomew's Drawing Books. 6.
Warren's Primary Geography. 7. Kerl's Elementary
English Grammar.

Same.   *Class* 2. — No. 1. Spelling. 2. Hillard's Fifth
Reader. 3. Writing, as in Fourth Class. 4. Eaton's
Intellectual Arithmetic, and Eaton's Common School
Arithmetic, revised edition. 5. Warren's Common
School Geography, with exercises in Map Drawing,
on the blackboard, and by pen and pencil. 6. Kerl's
Elementary English Grammar, or Kerl's Comprehen-
sive English Grammar. 7. Drawing in Bartholomew's
Drawing Books. 8. Exercises in Composition, and,

in the boys' schools, Declamation. 9. Swan's First
Lessons in the History of the United States.

Class 1. — No. 1. Spelling. — Adams's Spelling Book Text books.
for advanced classes, *permitted*. 2. Reading in Hillard's
Sixth Reader. 3. Writing as in Fourth Class. 4.
Geography, as in Class Two. 5. Eaton's Intellectual
Arithmetic, and Eaton's Common School Arithmetic,
revised edition. 6. Grammar. 7. Exercises in Composition, and in the boys' schools, in Declamation. 8.
Drawing in Bartholomew's Drawing Books. 9. Worcester's Dictionary. 10. Book-keeping by single entry.
11. Worcester's History. 12. Hall's Manual of Morals,
— a Monday morning lesson, with oral instruction. 13.
Instruction in Natural Philosophy, using Hooker's
Natural Philosophy, as a text book, with the Philosophical Apparatus provided for the schools, shall be given
at least to the first division of the First Class. 14. Instruction in Physical Geography, by occasional exercises ;
the treatise of Warren, or of Cartée, being used as a
text-book. 15. Hooker's Primary Philosophy.

SECT. 10. In teaching Arithmetic to the several Permitted
classes, every teacher shall be at liberty to employ such books.
books as he shall deem useful, for the purpose of afford-
ing illustration and examples ; but such books shall not
be used to the exclusion or neglect of the prescribed
text-books ; nor shall the pupils be required to furnish
themselves with any book but the text-books.

SECT. 11. One treatise on Mental Arithmetic, and Text-books.
one treatise on Written Arithmetic, and no more, shall
be used as text-books in the Grammar Schools.

SECT. 12. Two half-hours each week in the Gram- Instruction in
mar Schools shall be devoted to the study and practice music.

of Vocal Music. Instruction shall be given to the First and Second Classes by the music teachers. Musical notation, the singing of the scale, and exercises in reading simple music shall be practised twice a week by the lower classes under the direction of the assistant teach-

Examination in music. ers; and the pupils shall undergo examinations and receive credits for proficiency in music, as in the other studies pursued in the schools.

Arrangement of the studies and recitations. SECT. 13. It is recommended that in the arrangement of the studies and recitations in the Grammar Schools, those which most severely task the attention and effort of the pupils be, as far as possible, assigned for the forenoon.

Committees to superintend the organization of the first class. SECT. 14. It shall be the duty of the Committee of each Grammar School, at the beginning of each school year, either at a special meeting called for this purpose, or through their chairman, previously authorized to act in their name, to superintend the organization of the

No pupils to be retained who should join the High Schools. first class, and to see that none are retained members thereof who ought to join the English High School, or the Girls' High and Normal School.

CHAPTER XI.

Regulations of the English High School.

English High School established, and its object. SECTION 1. This school is situated in Bedford Street. It was instituted in 1821, with the design of furnishing the young men of the city who are not intended for a collegiate course of studies, and who have enjoyed the usual advantages of the other Public Schools, with the means of completing a good English education, and fit-

ing themselves for all the departments of commercial
life. The prescribed course of studies is arranged for
three years, and those who attend for that period and
complete that course, are considered to have been gradu-
ated at the school. Those who wish to pursue further
some of the higher departments of mathematics, and
other branches, have the privilege of remaining another
year at school. This institution is furnished with a valu-
able mathematical and philosophical apparatus, for the
purpose of experiment and illustration. To this school
apply the following regulations, in addition to those common to all the schools.

SECT. 2. The instructors in this school shall be a Instructors.
master, two sub-masters, and as many ushers as shall
allow one instructor to every thirty-five pupils, but no
additional usher shall be allowed for a less number. The
Sub-Committee may furnish the master with an assistant
in his room whenever the number of pupils remaining
in the school through the fourth year shall in their judgment make it necessary. The salary of said assistant
shall not exceed the salary paid to an usher in this
school during his first year of service. It shall be a
necessary qualification in all these instructors that they
have been educated at some respectable college, and that
they be competent to instruct in the French language.

SECT. 3. Candidates for admission to this school shall Time of exam-
be examined once a year, on the Wednesday and Thurs- ining candi-
day next succeeding the exhibition of the Grammar mission.
Schools in July. Any boy then offering himself as a
candidate for admission, shall present a certificate from
his parent and guardian that he has reached the age of
twelve years, also a certificate of good moral character,
and of presumed literary qualifications, from the master
of the school which he last attended, and shall pass a

satisfactory examination in the following studies, viz:
Spelling, Reading, Writing, English Grammar, Arithmetic, Modern Geography, and the History of the United
States.

Annual examination of candidates.

Sect. 4. It shall be the duty of the Committee on
the English High School to be present at the annual
examination of candidates for admission, but said examination shall be conducted by the instructors, from questions previously prepared, on all the branches, and subject to the approval of the Committee. The examination
shall be strict; and a thorough knowledge of the required studies shall be indispensable to admission.

Sect. 5. On admission, pupils shall be arranged in
divisions according to their respective degrees of proficiency. Individuals, however, shall be advanced according to their scholarship, and no faster; and no one shall
remain a member of the school longer than four years.

Reviews.

Sect. 6. It shall be the duty of the master to examine each division as often as may be consistent with the
attention due to those under his immediate instruction.
Each class or section shall be occasionally reviewed in
its appropriate studies, and once a quarter there shall be
a general review of all the previous studies of that
quarter.

School hours.

Sect. 7. The school shall hold one session, daily,
commencing at 9 A. M. and closing at 2 P. M., except
on Saturday, when the school shall close at 1 o'clock.

Course of studies and text-books.

Sect. 8. The course of study and instruction in this
school shall be as follows : —

Class 3. 1. Review of preparatory studies, using the
text-books authorized in the Grammar Schools of the
city. 2. Ancient Geography. 3. Worcester's General
History. 4. Sherwin's Algebra. 5. French Language.
6. Drawing.

Class 2. 1. Sherwin's Algebra, continued. 2. French sam. Language, continued. 3. Drawing, continued. 4. Legendre's Geometry. 5. Book-keeping. 6. Blair's Rhetoric. 7. Constitution of the United States. 8. Trigonometry, with its application to Surveying, Navigation, Mensuration, Astronomical Calculations, &c. 9. Paley's Evidences of Christianity,— a Monday morning lesson.

Class 1.   Trigonometry, with its applications, &c., Same. continued. 2. Paley's Evidences, continued, — a Monday morning lesson. 3. Drawing, continued. 4. Astronomy. 5. Natural Philosophy. 6. Moral Philosophy. 7. Political Economy. 8. Natural Theology. 9. Shaw's Lectures on English Literature. 10. French, continued, — or the Spanish Language may be commenced by such pupils as in the judgment of the master have acquired a competent knowledge of the French, Warren's Treatise on Physical Geography, or Cartée's Physical Geography and Atlas, is *permitted* to be used.

For the pupils who remain at the school the fourth year, the course of studies shall be as follows : —

1. Astronomy. 2. Intellectual Philosophy. 3. Logic. Same. 4. Spanish. 5. Geology. 6. Chemistry. 7. Mechanics, Engineering and the higher Mathematics, with some option.

SECT. 9.   The several classes shall also have exer- Same. cises in English Composition and Declamation. The instructors shall pay particular attention to the penmanship of the pupils, and give constantly such instruction in Spelling, Reading, and English Grammar, as they may deem necessary to make the pupils familiar with these fundamental branches of a good education.

H

Diplomas to
graduates.

Sect. 10.   Each pupil who shall graduate from this
school, having honorably completed its course of instruction to the satisfaction of the Principal and the Committee, shall be entitled to receive a suitable diploma on
leaving school.

CHAPTER XII.

Regulations of the Girls' High and Normal School.

Establishment
and object of
the school.

Section 1.   This school is situated in Mason Street.
It was instituted in 1852, with the design of furnishing
to those pupils who have passed through the usual
course of studies at the Grammar Schools for girls, and
at other girls' schools in this city, an opportunity for a
higher and more extended education, and also to fit
such of them as desire to become teachers.   The following are the regulations of this school, in addition to
those common to all the schools.

Instructors.

Sect. 2.   The instructors shall be, a master, and as
many assistants as may be found expedient; but the
whole number of assistants shall not exceed the ratio of
one for every thirty pupils.*

* At a meeting of the School Committee held May 17, 1864, the following
Orders were passed: —

1. Ordered, That the Committee on the Girls' High and Normal School be
authorized to employ a special instructor in the Normal Department of that
School, with a salary not exceeding $800 per annum.

2. Ordered, That those members of the Senior Class in the Girls' High and
Normal School who intend to become teachers, shall be required to attend the
sessions of one or more of the Primary and Grammar Schools in the city, not
less than four weeks during the year, in order to observe the methods of
teaching, and to acquire practical knowledge of the instruction and government of school, by acting as teachers themselves; — it being understood that
they are to be under the supervision and direction of the Chairman of the District Committee, and of the master, of the school in which they are employed,
and that they are to receive no remuneration.

Sect. 3. The examination of candidates for admis- Admission of sion to the schools, shall take place annually, on the pupils. Wednesday and Thursday next succeeding the day of the annual exhibition of the Grammar Schools in July.

Sect. 4. Candidates for admission must be over fif- Same. teen, and not more than nineteen years of age. They must present certificates of recommendation from the teachers whose schools they last attended, and must pass a satisfactory examination in the following branches, viz : Spelling, Reading, Writing, Arithmetic, English Grammar, Geography, and History.

Sect. 5. The examination shall be conducted by the Same. instructors of the school, both orally and from written questions previously prepared by them, and approved by the Committee of the school. It shall be the duty of the said Committee to be present and to assist at the examination, and the admission of candidates shall be subject to their approval.

Sect. 6. The course of studies and instruction in Course of instruction. this school shall be as follows : —

Junior Class. Reading, Spelling, and Writing, continued. Arithmetic, Geography, and Grammar, reviewed. Physical Geography, Natural Philosophy, Analysis of Language and Structure of Sentences. Synonymes. Rhetoric. Exercises in English Composition. History. Latin, begun. Exercises in Drawing and in Vocal Music.

Middle Class. Natural Philosophy, continued. English Literature. Algebra. Moral Philosophy. Latin, continued. French, begun (instruction given by a native French teacher). Rhetoric, with exercises in Composition, continued. Physiology, with Lectures. General History. Exercises in Drawing and in Vocal Music.

Reading standard English Works, with exercises in Criticism.

Senior Class. Latin and French, continued. Geometry. General History. Intellectual Philosophy. Astronomy. Chemistry, with lectures. Exercises in Composition. Exercises in Drawing and in Vocal Music. Exercises in Criticism, comprising a careful examination of works of the best English authors. Instruction in the theory and Practice of Teaching. Such instruction in Music shall be given to all the pupils as may qualify them to teach Vocal Music in our Public Schools.

School hours. SECT. 7. The sessions of the schools shall begin at 9 o'clock, A. M. and close at 2 o'clock, P. M., except on Wednesday and Saturday, when the school shall close at 1 o'clock.

Visitations by parents and friends. SECT. 8. Instead of a public exhibition in this school the parents and friends of the pupils shall be invited through the pupils to attend the regular exercises in the various rooms during the five days preceding the last school-day of the school year. And during such visitations the exercises of the school shall be conducted in the usual manner.

Pupils may remain three years. SECT. 9. The plan of study shall be arranged for three years. Pupils who have attended for that period, and who have completed the course in a manner satisfactory to the teachers and the Committee on the school, Diploma. shall be entitled to receive a diploma or certificate to that effect, on leaving school.

CHAPTER XIII.

Regulations of the Latin Grammar School.

SECTION 1. This school, situated in Bedford Street, was instituted early in the 17th century.

SECT. 2. The rudiments of the Latin and Greek lan- *Objects of the schools.* guages are taught, and scholars are fitted for the most respectable colleges. Instruction is also given in Mathematics, Geography, History, Declamation, English Grammar, Composition, and in the French language. The following Regulations, in addition to those common to all the schools, apply to this school.

SECT. 3. The instructors in this school shall be a *Instructors.* master, a sub-master, and as many ushers as shall allow one instructor to every thirty-five pupils, and no additional usher shall be allowed for a less number.

SECT. 4. It shall be a necessary qualification for the *Same.* instructors of this school, that they shall have been educated at a college of good standing.

SECT. 5. Each candidate for admission shall have *Candidates for admission.* attained the age of ten years, and shall produce from the master of the school he last attended, a certificate of good moral character. He shall be able to read English correctly and fluently, to spell all words of common occurrence, to write a running hand, understand Mental Arithmetic and the simple rules of Written Arithmetic, and be able to answer the most important questions in Geography, and shall have a sufficient knowledge of English Grammar to parse common sentences in prose. A knowledge of Latin Grammar shall be considered equivalent to that of English.

Time of examining candidates for admission.

Sect. 6. Boys shall be examined for admission to this school only once a year, viz: on the Friday and Saturday of the last week of the vacation succeeding the exhibition of the school in July.

Pupils may remain six years.

Sect. 7. The regular course of instruction shall continue six years, and no scholar shall enjoy the privileges of this school beyond that term, unless by written leave of the Committee. But scholars may have the option of completing their course in five years or less time, if willing to make due exertions, and shall be advanced according to scholarship.

School hours.

Sect. 8. The sessions of the school shall begin at 9 o'clock A. M. and close at 2 o'clock P. M. on every school-day throughout the year, except on Saturday, when the school shall close at 1 o'clock.

Classes.

Sect. 9. The school shall be divided into classes and subdivisions, as the master, with the approbation of the Committee, may think advisable.

Sect. 10. The master shall examine the pupils under the care of the other teachers in the school as often as he can consistently with proper attention to those in his own charge.

Course of studies and text-books.

Sect. 11. The books and exercises required in the course of instruction in this school, are the following : —

Class 6. 1. Andrews and Stoddard's Latin Grammar. 2. English Grammar. 3. Reading English. 4. Spelling. 5. Mental Arithmetic. 6. Mitchell's Geographical Questions. 7. Declamation. 8. Penmanship. 9. Andrews's Latin Lessons. 10. Andrews's Latin Reader.

Class 5. 1, 2, 3, 4, 7, 8, continued. 11. Viri Romæ. 12. Written translations. 13. Colburn's Sequel. 14. Cornelius Nepos. 15. Arnold's Latin Prose Composition.

Class 4.   1, 2, 3, 4, 7, 8, 12, 13, 15, continued.
16. Sophocles's Greek Grammar.   17. Sophocles's Greek
Lessons.   18. Cæsar's Commentaries.   19. Fasquelle's
French Grammar.   20. Exercises in speaking and reading French with a native French teacher.

 Class 3.   1, 2, 3, 4, 7, 8, 12, 13, 15, 16, 19, 20, ^{Text books.}
continued.   21. Ovid's Metamorphoses.   22. Arnold's
Greek Prose Composition.   23. Felton's Greek Reader.
24. Sherwin's Algebra.   25. English Composition.   26.
Le Grandpere.

 Class 2.   1, 2, 3, 4, 7, 8, 15, 16, 19, 21, 22, 23, ^{Same.}
24, 25, continued.   27. Virgil.   28. Elements of History.   29. Translations from English into Latin.

 Class 1.   1, 7, 15, 16, 19, 20, 21, 22, 23, 25, ^{Same.}
27, 28, 29, continued.   30. Geometry.   31. Cicero's
Orations.   32. Composition of Latin Verses.   33.
Composition in French.   34. Ancient History and
Geography.

 The following books of reference may be used in pur- ^{Same.}
suing the above studies : —

Leverett's Latin Lexicon, or Gardner's abridgment
of the same.

Andrews's Latin Lexicon.

Liddell and Scott's Greek Lexicon, or Pickering's
Greek Lexicon, last edition.

Worcester's School Dictionary.

Smith's Classical Dictionary.

Smith's Dictionary of Antiquities.

Baird's Classic Manual.   Warren's Treatise on Physical Geography, or Cartee's Physical Geography and
Atlas is *permitted* to be used.

 SECT. 12.   No Translations, nor any Interpretation,
Keys, or Orders of Construction, are allowed in the
school.

Sect. 13.   The instructors shall pay particular attention to the penmanship of the pupils, and give constantly
such instruction in Spelling, Reading, and English
Grammar, as they may deem necessary to make the pupils familiar with those fundamental branches of a good
education.

Diploma or
certificate.

Sect. 14.   Each pupil who shall honorably complete
the course of studies prescribed for this school, to the
satisfaction of the Principal and the Committee, shall be
entitled to receive a suitable diploma or certificate to that
effect at graduation.

BOUNDARIES

OF THE

GRAMMAR SCHOOL SECTIONS.

Adams School, for Boys and Girls.

Comprises that portion of East Boston lying south and east of a line running from the Bay on the east, through Porter Street to the railroad, thence along the railroad to Decatur Street, through Decatur to Chelsea Street, through Chelsea to Elbow Street, through Elbow to Meridian Street, through Meridian to Maverick Street, through Maverick to Havre Street, through Havre Street to the water.

Bigelow School for Boys and Girls.

Comprises all that part of South Boston lying between the sections of the Lawrence and the Lincoln School.

Bowditch School, for Girls.

Commencing at the foot of State Street, through State, Washington, Summer, and Kingston streets, to the Worcester Railroad; thence by the railroad to its junction with Albany Street; thence by a line drawn at right angle with Albany Street, to the water; thence by the water to the bound first named.

Bowdoin School, for Girls.

Commencing at Cambridge Bridge, thence by the centre of Cambridge Street to Staniford Street, thence through the centre

1

of Staniford to Green Street, thence across Green Street and through the centre of Lyman Place to Prospect Street, thence through the centre of Prospect to Causeway Street, thence through the centre of Causeway Street to the Boston and Maine Railroad, thence by said railroad to Haymarket Square, thence through the centre of Haymarket Square to Portland Street, thence through the centre of Portland to Sudbury Street, thence through the centre of Sudbury to Court Street, thence through the centre of Court to Washington Street, through Washington to West Street, thence across the Common to the Milldam, including the tenements on both sides of the Milldam road, and thence by the water to the bound first named.

Boylston School, for Boys.

Commencing at the water opposite Federal Street, thence through Federal, including both sides, to Milk Street, thence through the centre of Milk to Congress Street, thence through the centre of Congress to State Street, thence through the centre of State Street to the water, thence by the water to the bound first named.

Brimmer School, for Boys.

Includes all that portion of Boston which lies west of the centre of Washington Street, between the centre of Dedham Street and the centres of School and Beacon streets.

Chapman School, for Boys and Girls.

Comprises that portion of East Boston lying north of a line commencing at the Mystic River and running easterly through Central Square and Porter Street, along its continuation, to the Bay on the east.

Dwight School, for Boys.

Includes all of Boston south of the centre of Dedham Street.

Eliot School, for Boys.

Beginning at the water at the foot of Richmond Street, thence through the centre of Richmond to Salem Street, thence by the centre of Salem to Cooper Street, thence by the centre of Cooper to Beverly Street, thence by the centre of Beverly, and in the same direction with Beverly Street, to the water, thence by the water to the point begun at.

Everett School, for Girls.

Includes all of Boston south of the centre of Dedham Street.

Franklin School, for Girls.

Includes all that portion of Boston which lies between the centre of Dedham Street on the south, and the Worcester Railroad and a line drawn from its junction with Albany Street to the water on the north.

Hancock School, for Girls.

Commencing on the Maine Railroad at the water, thence by the railroad to Haymarket Square, through the centre of Haymarket Square to Portland Street, through the centre of Portland to Sudbury Street, through the centre of Sudbury to Court Street, through the centre of Court to State Street, through the centre of State Street to the water, thence by the water to the Maine Railroad, the bound first named.

Lawrence School, for Boys and Girls.

Comprises all that part of South Boston west and northwest of D Street.

Lincoln School, for Boys and Girls.

Includes all that part of South Boston east of Old Harbor Street, and of a line running through the centre of Fifth and F streets to the shore of Boston Harbor.

Lyman School, for Boys and Girls.

Commencing at the Mystic River and running easterly through Central Square and Porter Street to the railroad, thence along the railroad through Decatur, Chelsea, Elbow, Meridian, Maverick, and Havre streets to the water, thence by the water to the bound first named.

Mayhew School, for Boys.

Commencing at the foot of Leverett Street, at Cragie's Bridge, thence through the centre of Leverett to Green Street, thence through the centre of Green to Chambers Street, thence through the centre of Chambers to Cambridge Street, thence across Cambridge and through the centre of Joy Street to Beacon Street, thence through the centre of Beacon and School streets to Washington Street, thence through the centre of Washington to State Street, thence through the centre of State Street to the water, thence by the water to the foot of Richmond Street, thence by the centre of Richmond to Salem Street, thence by the centre of Salem to Cooper Street, thence by the centre of Cooper Street to Beverly Street, thence by the centre of Beverly, and in the same direction with Beverly Street, to the water, thence by the water to the point begun at.

Phillips School, for Boys.

Commencing at the Milldam, thence by the centre of Beacon to Joy Street, thence through the centre of Joy to Cambridge Street, thence across Cambridge Street, and through the centre of Chambers and Green streets to Leverett Street, thence through the centre of Leveret Street to Cragie's Bridge, and thence by the water to the bound first named, including the tenements on both sides of the Milldam.

Quincy School, for Boys.

Includes all that portion of Boston lying between the centre of Dedham Street and the centre of State Street, bounded on the west by the centre of Washington Street, and on the east by a line running through the centres of Congress, Milk, Federal, excluding both sides, and Summer streets, and by the water.

Wells School, for Girls.

Commencing at the water on the easterly end of Cambridge Bridge, thence by the water to the Boston and Maine Railroad, thence by said railroad to Causeway Street, thence by the centre of Causeway to Prospect Street, thence by the centre of Prospect Street to Lyman Place, thence by the centre of Lyman Place to Green Street, thence across Green and through the centre of Staniford to Cambridge Street, thence by the centre of Cambridge Street to the bound first named.

Winthrop School, for Girls.

Commencing at the water near the Milldam, thence across the Common to West Street, through the centre of West to Washington Street, through the centre of Washington to Summer Street, through the centre of Summer and Kingston streets, to the Worcester Railroad, thence by the railroad, to the bound first named.

INDEX.

ORGANIZATION

OF THE

PUBLIC SCHOOLS.

L

SCHOOL COMMITTEE

FOR 1865.

FREDERIC W. LINCOLN, JR., MAYOR, *ex officio.*

WM. B. FOWLE, JR. PRESIDENT OF THE COMMON COUNCIL, *ex officio.*

TERM EXPIRES JAN. 1866.	TERM EXPIRES JAN. 1867.	TERM EXPIRES JAN. 1868.
WARD		
1.— George F. Haskins, Horace Dodd.	Benjamin Fessenden, Charles A. Turner.	William A. Kreuger, Joseph D. Fallon.
2.— Samuel T. Cobb, Seth C. Ames.	Edwin Wright, Bradford L. Crocker.	Warren H. Cudworth, J. Harvey Woodbury.
3.— Aaron P. Richardson, George Hubbard.	Aurelius L. Weymouth, Timothy H. Smith.	Benjamin T. Gould, Michael Leary.
4.— Dexter S. King, John A. Lamson.	Nathaniel B. Shurtleff, Ezra Palmer.	Edward D. G. Palmer, Orrin S. Sanders.
5.— William C. Williamson, Henry Warren.	Samuel H. Winkley, Robert I. Burbank.	John F. Jarvis, Warren S. Beal.
6.— Samuel K. Lothrop, Henry W. Haynes.	Henry Burroughs, Jr. Loring Lothrop.	J. Baxter Upham, Calvin G. Page.
7.— Patrick Riley, George Hayward.	Michael Moran, M. Field Fowler.	John P. Ordway, Charles Butler.
8.— Elijah C. Drew, Edmund T. Eastman.	Dio Lewis, Charles H. Spring.	Thomas M. Brewer, William H. Page.
9.— Elisha Bassett, Charles Torrey.	Joseph L. Drew, William E. Underwood.	Jacob M. Manning, M. Denman Ross.
10.— Stephen L. Emery, Henry W. Harrington.	Charles Edward Cook, Ira L. Moore.	Enoch C. Rolfe, Salem T. Lamb.
11.— Wm. H. Learnard, Jr. Matthias Rich.	Alden Speare, Charles W. Slack.	Robert C. Waterston, Benjamin W. Williams.
12.— J. Proctor Haskins, Edward H. Brainard.	Edwin Briggs, Nathaniel Hayes.	Henry A. Drake, Francis H. Underwood.

JOHN D. PHILBRICK, *Superintendent of Public Schools.*

BARNARD CAPEN, *Secretary of School Committee.*

ORGANIZATION

OF THE

BOARD OF SCHOOL COMMITTEE.

--- --- ---

STANDING COMMITTEES.

COMMITTEE ON ELECTIONS.

Messrs. Joseph L. Drew, 52 Warren Street.
Benjamin Fessenden, 25 Charter Street.
Edward H. Brainard, 161 Broadway.
Stephen L. Emery, 603 Tremont Street.
William C. Williamson, 23 McLean Street.

COMMITTEE ON RULES AND REGULATIONS.

Messrs. William H. Learnard, Jr., 61 Rutland Street.
George F. Haskins, 2 North Square.
George Hayward, 13 Temple Place.
Elisha Bassett, 335 Tremont Street.
Henry A. Drake, 333 Broadway.

COMMITTEE ON SALARIES.

Messrs. Charles W. Slack, 10 Garland Street.
Loring Lothrop, 43 Pinckney Street.
Edmund T. Eastman, 50 Essex Street.
M. Field Fowler, 25 South Street.
J. Harvey Woodbury, 4 Princeton Street.

COMMITTEE ON ACCOUNTS.

Messrs. Enoch C. Rolfe, 616 Washington Street,
Elijah C. Drew, 40 State Street.
Samuel T. Cobb, 27 Cornhill.
Patrick Riley, 10 Lincoln Street.
Salem T. Lamb, 10 Burroughs Place.

COMMITTEE ON TEXT-BOOKS.

Messrs. S. K. Lothrop, 12 Chestnut Street.
Henry Burroughs, Jr., 82 Mount Vernon Street.
Ezra Palmer, 1 Tremont Place.
John F. Jarvis, 22 Leverett Street.
John A. Lamson, 1 Staniford Street.

COMMITTEE ON SCHOOLHOUSES.

Messrs. William E. Underwood, 743 Washington Street.
Nathaniel B. Shurtleff, 2 Beacon Street.
Thomas M. Brewer, 131 Washington Street.
Charles Edward Cook, 220 Washington Street.
Edwin Wright, 9 Joy's Building.

COMMITTEE ON MUSIC.

Messrs. J. Baxter Upham, 31 Chestnut Street.
Aaron P. Richardson, 17 Green Street.
John P. Ordway, 42 Bedford Street.
Francis H. Underwood, 282 Fourth Street.
Robert C. Waterston, 71 Chester Square.

COMMITTEE ON PRINTING.

Messrs. Henry W. Harrington, 3 Corey Avenue.
Dexter S. King, 34 Bowdoin Street.
J. Proctor Haskins, Seventh, near E Street.
Warren S. Beal, 2 Blossom Court.
Benjamin W. Williams, 36 Clarendon Street.

Messrs. George Hayward, 13 Temple Place.
Edward H. Brainard, 161 Broadway.
J. Baxter Upham, 31 Chestnut Street.
Robert I. Burbank, 8 Staniford Street.
William B. Fowle, 7 W. Chester Park.

LATIN AND HIGH SCHOOLS.

PUBLIC LATIN SCHOOL, BEDFORD STREET.

COMMITTEE.

Nathaniel B. Shurtleff, *Chairman*, 2 Beacon Street.
Francis H. Underwood, *Secretary*, 2½2 Fourth Street.
William B. Fowle, 7 West Chester Park.
George F. Haskins, 2 North Square.
Edwin Wright, 9 Joy's Building.
Aurelius L. Weymouth, 9 Green Street.
Samuel H. Winkley, 5 Chambers Street.
Henry W. Haynes, 35 Court Street.
John P. Ordway, 42 Bedford Street.
Edmund T. Eastman, 50 Essex Street.
Jacob M. Manning, 9 Boylston Place.
Charles Edward Cook, 220 Washington Street.
Charles W. Slack, 10 Garland Street.

Francis Gardner, *Master*,
Edward H. Magill, *Sub-Master*.
William R. Dimmock, *Sub-Master*.
Charles J. Capen, Moses Merrill, Joseph A. Hale, and Albert Palmer,
   Ushers.
Edward Coquard, *Teacher of French*.

ENGLISH HIGH SCHOOL, BEDFORD STREET.

COMMITTEE.

S. K. Lothrop, *Chairman*, 12 Chestnut Street.
Salem T. Lamb, *Secretary*, 10 Burroughs Place.
William B. Fowle, 7 West Chester Park.
Charles A. Turner, 364 Hanover Street.
Warren H. Cudworth, 1 Meridian Street.
Benjamin T. Gould, 1 Prospect Street.
Dexter S. King, 34 Bowdoin Street.
Henry Warren, 25 Green Street.
Patrick Riley, 10 Lincoln Street.
Elijah C. Drew, 40 State Street.
William E. Underwood, 743 Washington Street.
Robert C. Waterston, 71 Chester Square.
Henry A. Drake, 333 Broadway.

Thomas Sherwin, *Master*.
Charles M. Cumston, *First Sub-Master*.
Luther W. Anderson, *Second Sub-Master*.
Ephraim Hunt, William Nichols, Jr., Robert E. Babson, *Ushers*.
William N. Bartholomew, *Teacher of Drawing*.

GIRLS' HIGH AND NORMAL SCHOOL,

MASON STREET.

COMMITTEE.

Henry Burroughs, Jr., *Chairman*, 82 Mount Vernon Street.
John F. Jarvis, *Secretary*, 22 Leverett Street.
William B. Fowle, 7 West Chester Park.
Benjamin Fessenden, 22 Charter Street.
Samuel T. Cobb, 2 Belmont Square.
Aaron P. Richardson, 17 Green Street.
Ezra Palmer, 1 Tremont Place.
George Hayward, 13 Temple Place.
Thomas M. Brewer, 131 Washington Street.
Elisha Bassett, 335 Tremont Street.
Enoch C. Rolfe, 616 Washington Street.
Alden Speare, 15 E. Brookline Street.
Edwin Briggs, 67 Dorchester Street.

William H. Seavey, *Master.*
Harriet E. Caryl, *Head Assistant.*
Jane H. Stickney, *Superintendent of Training Department.*
Sarah D. Duganne, *Assistant Training Department.*

ASSISTANTS.

Maria A. Bacon,	Mary E. Scates,
Margaret A. Badger,	Adeline L. Sylvester,
Helen W. Avery,	Mary H. Ellis,
Emma A. Temple,	Frances A. Poole,
Catharine Knapp,	Elizabeth C. Light,

William N. Bartholomew, *Teacher of Drawing.*
Carl Zerrahn, *Teacher of Music.*
Philip Wilner, *Teacher of German.*
Edward Coquard, *Teacher of French.*

THE SCHOOL DISTRICTS,

ARRANGED IN ALPHABETICAL ORDER.

———   .

ADAMS SCHOOL DISTRICT.

COMMITTEE.

Seth C. Ames, *Chairman*, 131 Webster Street.
Samuel T. Cobb, *Secretary*, 2 Belmont Square.
Edwin Wright, 134 Lexington Street.
Bradford L. Crocker, 124 Webster Street.
Timothy H. Smith, 82 Salem Street.
J. Harvey Woodbury, 4 Princeton Street.
Warren H. Cudworth, 1 Meridian Street.

ADAMS SCHOOL, BELMONT SQUARE, EAST BOSTON.

Robert C. Metcalf, *Master*,
  Cl. I., Div. 1, Room 14,
Frank F. Preble, *Sub-Master*,
  Cl. I., Div. 2, Room 8.

Jane S. Tower, *Head Assistant*,
  Master's Room.
Margaret J. Allison, *Head Assistant*,
  Cl. II., Div. 1, Girls. Room 12.
Louisa E. Harris, *Head Assistant*,
  Cl. II., Div 1, Boys. Room 4.

Assistants.

Martha E. Webb,
  Cl. III., Div. 1, Boys. Room 6.
Juliette J. Pierce,
  Cl. III., Div. 2, Boys. Room 7.
Josephine J. Longley,
  Cl. III., Div. 1, Girls. Room 10.

Mary M. Morse,
  Cl. IV., Div. 1, Boys. Room 5.
Almira G. Smith,
  Cl. IV., Div. 1, Girls. Room 1.
Sarah J. D'Arcy,
  Cl. IV., Div. 2, Boys. Room 3.
Lucy A. Wiggin,
  Cl. IV., Div. 2, Girls. Room 2.

Eunice H. C. Culver, *Teacher of Sewing.*
——— ———, *Instructor in Music.*

PRIMARY SCHOOLS.

Teachers.	Location.	Sub-Committees.
Emily C. Morse,	No. 1 — Sumner Street,	
Rosa L. Morse,	2 " "	
Eliza A. Wiggin,	Adams Schoolhouse,	
Mary L. McLoud,	" "	Messrs. Cobb & Smith.
Mary E. Morse,	" "	
Esther L. Morse,	" "	
Elizabeth Lincoln,	1 — Webster Street.	
Mary H. Allen,	2 " "	Messrs. Ames & Smith.
Susan D. Wilde.	3 " "	

BIGELOW SCHOOL DISTRICT.

COMMITTEE.

Henry A. Drake, *Chairman*, 333 Broadway.
Nathaniel Hayes, *Secretary*, E Street, cor. Broadway.
J. Proctor Haskins, 8 Woodward Street.
Edwin Briggs, 67 Dorchester Street.
Edward H. Brainard, 161 Broadway.
Francis H. Underwood, 282 Fourth Street.
William H. Page, 48 Beach Street.

BIGELOW SCHOOL, FOURTH STREET, SOUTH BOSTON.

Charles Goodwin Clark, *Master*,
Cl. I., Div. 1, Room 1.
Thomas H. Barnes, *Sub-Master*,
Cl. I., Div. 1, Room 9.

Rachel C. Mather, *Head Assistant*,
Cl. II., Div. 1, Room 4.
Mary A. Currier, *Head Assistant*,
Cl. I., Div. 1, Room 1.
Celinda Seaver, *Head Assistant*,
Cl. IV., Div. 1, Room 11.

Assistants.

Sarah E. Fisher,
Cl. II., Div. 1, Room 2.
Mary A. Hale,
Cl. II., Div. 2, Room 5.
Lydia E. Tonkin,
Cl. III., Div. 1, Room 6.
Lucinda P. Works,
Cl. III., Div. 2, Room 3.
Roxanna M. Blanchard,
Cl. III., Div. 4, Room 7.

Lavinia B. Pendleton,
Cl. III., Div. 5, Room 10.
Florence W. Stetson,
Cl. III., Div. 2, Room 8.
Julia Clapp,
Cl. IV., Div. 2, Room 14.
Elizabeth Williams,
Cl. IV. Div. 3, Room 13.
Clara E. Farrington,
Cl. IV. Div. 4, Room 12.

Washington Village Branch.
Harriet S. Howes,
Cl. IV., Divs. 1, 2, and 3.

Henrietta M. Whiton, *Teacher of Sewing.*
Joseph B. Sharland, *Teacher of Music.*

PRIMARY SCHOOLS.

Teachers.	*Location.*	*Sub-Committee.*
Martha C. Jenks,	No. 1 — Hawes Hall,	Haskins and Brainard.
Mary P. Colburn,	2 " "	Haskins and Hayes.
Ann Jane Lyon,	4 " "	} Page and Briggs.
Lucy E. T. Tinkham,	5 " "	
Alice Danforth,	6 " "	Haskins and Hayes.
Anna C. Gill,	7 " "	Haskins and Brainard.
Caroline H. Holder,	8 " "	Page and Briggs.
Sarah A. Graham,	1 — Lyceum Hall,	Haskins and Brainard.
Josephine B. Cherrington,	2 " "	Page and Briggs.
Maria A. Cook,	Washington Village,	} Briggs and Underwood.
Emeline L. Tolman,	" "	
——— ———,	" "	
Harriet A. Clapp,	Mattapan Hall,	Haskins and Brainard.
Mary L. Howard,	Rear of Hawes Hall,	Page and Briggs.

BOWDITCH SCHOOL DISTRICT.

COMMITTEE.

Henry W. Haynes, *Chairman,* 35 Court Street.
M. Field Fowler, *Secretary,* 25 South Street.
Thomas M. Brewer, 131 Washington Street.
Patrick Riley, 10 Lincoln Street.
John P. Ordway, 42 Bedford Street.
George Hayward, 13 Temple Place.
Michael Moran, 73 Purchase Street.
William H. Page, 48 Beach Street.
Dio Lewis, 20 Essex Street
John A. Lamson, 1 Staniford Street.

BOWDITCH SCHOOL, SOUTH STREET.

William T. Adams, *Master*,
  Cl. I., Div. 1.
Caroline L. G. Badger, *Head Ass't*,
  Master's Room.

Clarinda R. F. Treadwell, *Head Ass't*,
  Cl. II., Div. 1.
Susan H. Thaxter, *Head Assistant*,
  Cl. III., Div. 1.
Sarah E. Daley, *Head Assistant*,
  Cl. IV., Div. 1.

Assistants.

Catherine S. Clinton,
  Cl. I., Div. 1.
Frances R. Honey,
  Cl. I., Div. 2.
Ellen M. S. Treadwell,
  Cl. II., Div. 2.
Ellen McKendry,
  Cl. II., Div. 3.
Ann Nowell,
  Cl. II., Div. 4.
Mary E. Nichols,
  Cl. III., Div. 2.

Caroline W. Marshall,
  Cl. III., Div. 3.
Mary M. T. Foley,
  Cl. III., Div. 4.
Annie B. Thompson,
  Cl. IV., Div. 2.
Rosalie Y. Abbott,
  Cl. IV., Div. 3.
Carolyn E. Jennison,
  Cl. IV., Div. 4.

Sarah A. Pope, *Assistant*,
  Cl. IV., Div. 5.

Georgiana M. L. Evert, *Assistant*,
  Cl. IV., Div. 6.

———— ————,
  Cl. IV., Div. 7.

Joseph B. Sharland, *Music Teacher.*
Eliza A. Baxter, *Sewing Teacher.*
Henry Farmer, *Janitor.*

PRIMARY SCHOOLS.

Teachers.	Location.	Sub-Committees.
Hannah E. G. Gleason,	No. 1 — High Street Place,	Mr. Moran.
Angelia M. Newmarch,	2 " " "	" Lamson,
Maria J. Coburn,	3 " " "	" Fowler.
Ruth H. Clapp,	4 " " "	" Page.
Octavia C. Heard,	5 " " "	" Hayward.
Mary G. Hillman,	6 " " "	" Ordway.
Harriette B. Cutler,	Belcher Lane,	" Riley.
H. Isabella Hopkins,	" "	" Brewer.
Celeste Weed,	Lane Place,	" Lewis.
Julia B. Lombard,	Purchase Place,	" Haynes.

BOWDOIN SCHOOL DISTRICT.

COMMITTEE.

John A. Lamson, *Chairman*, 1 Staniford Street.
Calvin G. Page, *Secretary*, 69 Myrtle Street.
Aaron P. Richardson, 17 Green Street.
Nathaniel B. Shurtleff, 2 Beacon Street.
J. Baxter Upham, 31 Chestnut Street.
Loring Lothrop, 43 Pinckney Street.
Ezra Palmer, 1 Tremont Place.
Orrin S. Sanders, 11 Bowdoin Street.
Robert I. Burbank, 8 Staniford Street.

BOWDOIN SCHOOL, MYRTLE STREET.

Daniel C. Brown, *Master*,

Deborah Norton, *2d Head Assistant*,
  Cl. I., Div. 2.

Sarah J. Mills, 1st *Head Assistant*,
  Cl. I., Div. 1.

Mary Young. 3d *Head Assistant*,
  Cl. I., Div. 3.

Assistants.

Emily G. Wetherbee,
  Cl. II., Div. 1.
Sophia B. Horr,
  Cl. II., Div. 2.
Eliza A. Fay,
  Cl. III., Div. 1.
Irene W. Wentworth,
  Cl. III., Div. 2.

Martha A. Palmer,
  Cl. III., Div. 3.
Lucy C. Gould,
  Cl. IV., Div. 1.
Mary F. Grant,
  Cl. IV., Div. 2.
Ann E. Kimball,
  Cl. IV., Div. 3.

——— ———, *Music Teacher.*

PRIMARY SCHOOLS.

Teachers.	Location.	Sub-Committees.
——— ———,	Somerset Street,	Mr. Lamson.
Albertina G. Porter,	" "	" Palmer.
C. Eliza Wason,	" "	" Richardson.
Charlotte A. Curtis,	Blossom Street,	" Sanders.
Olivie Ruggles,	" "	" Richardson.
Lydia A. Isbel,	" "	" Lothrop.
Louise J. Hovey,	" "	" Sanders.
——— ———,	Joy Street,	} " Page.
Helen M. Adams,	· Old Phillips Schoolhouse,	
Sarah E. Adams,	" " "	" Upham.
Marianne Stephens,	" " "	" Burbank.

BOYLSTON SCHOOL DISTRICT.

COMMITTEE.

Edmund T. Eastman, *Chairman*, 50 Essex Street.
John A. Lamson, *Secretary*, 1 Staniford Street.
Patrick Riley, 10 Lincoln Street.
John P. Ordway, 42 Bedford Street.
Charles Torrey, 105 Boylston Street.
M. Field Fowler, 25 South Street.
Michael Moran, 73 Purchase Street.
Charles Butler, 291 Washington Street.
Dio Lewis, 20 Essex Street.
Edward D. G. Palmer, 3 Montgomery Place.

BOYLSTON SCHOOL, FORT HILL.

Alfred Hewins, *Master*,
  Cl. I., Div. 1.
John Jameson, *Sub-Master*,
  Cl. I., Div. 2.

Henry H. Kimball, *Usher*,
  Cl. II., Div. 1.
Mary A. Davis, *Head Assistant*,
  Master's Room.

Assistants.

Sarah Fuller,
  Cl. II., Div. 2.
Mary L. Holland,
  Cl. III., Div. 1.
Josephine M. Hanna,
  Cl. III., Div. 2.
Susan B. Leeds,
  Cl. IV., Div. 1.

Jane M. Bullard,
  Cl. IV., Div. 2.
Caroline A. Morrill,
  Cl. IV., Div. 3.
Emily S. Hutchins,
  Cl. IV., Div. 4.
Annie M. Heustis,
  Cl. IV., Div. 5.

——— ———, *Music Teacher*.

PRIMARY SCHOOLS.

Teachers.	Location.		Sub-Committee.
Clara A. Clarke,	No. 1 — Lane Place.		Mr. Eastman.
Margaret F. Tappan,	2	" "	" Torrey.
Annie C. Haley,	3	" "	" Eastman.
Adelia E. Edwards,	4	" "	" Ordway.
Julia A. B. Gleason,	5	" "	" Fowler.
Ellen M. Perkins,	6	" "	" Lamson.
Mary E. Sawyer,	7	" "	" Butler.
Maria B. Clapp,	8	" "	" Moran.

Amelia E. N. Treadwell,	1 — Washington Square,	Mr. Torrey.
Anna M. Lecain,	2 " "	" Riley.
Ruth E. Rowe,	3 " "	" Fowler.
Julia A. O'Hara,	4 " "	" Ordway.
Mary L. G. Hanley,	5 " "	" Riley.
Lydia B. Felt,	6 " "	" Palmer.

BRIMMER SCHOOL DISTRICT.

COMMITTEE.

Charles Edward Cook, *Chairman*, 220 Washington Street,
Salem T. Lamb, *Secretary*, 10 Burroughs Place.
Elisha Bassett, 335 Tremont Street.
Henry W. Harrington, 3 Corey Avenue.
Enoch C. Rolfe, 616 Washington Street.
M. Denman Ross, 76 Boylston Street.
Charles Torrey, 105 Boylston Street.
Joseph L. Drew, 52 Warren Street.
Jacob M. Manning, 9 Boylston Place.

BRIMMER SCHOOL, COMMON STREET.

Joshua Bates, *Master*,
     Cl. I., Div. 1.
William L. P. Boardman, *Sub-Master*,
     Cl. I., Div. 2.
David A. Caldwell, *Usher*,
     Cl. I., Div. 3.

Rebecca L. Duncan, *Head Assistant*,
     Cl. I., Div. 1.
Mary E. Beck, *Head Assistant*,
     Cl. II., Div. 1.

Assistants.

Lavina E. Bunton,
     Cl. II., Div. 2.
Mercie T. Snow,
     Cl. II., Div. 3.
Luthera W. Bird,
     Cl. III., Div. 1.
Amanda Snow,
     Cl. III., Div. 2.

Harriet N. Lane,
     Cl. III., Div. 4.
Mercy A. Davie,
     Cl. IV., Div. 1.
Sarah J. March,
     Cl. IV., Div. 2.
Annie E. English,
     Cl. IV., Div. 3.

Annie P. James,
    Cl. III., Div. 3.

Susan P. Cunningham,
    Cl. IV., Div. 4.
Caroline B. Lerow,
    Cl. IV., Div. 5.
Joseph B. Sharland, *Music Teacher*.
Charles Gavett, *Janitor*.

PRIMARY SCHOOLS.

Teachers.	Location.	Sub-Committee.
Martha J. Coolidge,	No. 1 — Newbern Place,	Mr. Rolfe.
Dorcas B. Baldwin,	2 " "	" Lamb.
Catharine M. E. Richardson,	3 " "	" Ross.
Eliza F. Moriarty,	1 — Indiana Place,	} " Torrey.
Lucy H. Symonds,	2 " "	
Mary C. Willard,	1 — Nassau Hall,	" Rolfe.
Helen M. Dexter,	1 — Warren Street,	" Harrington.
Sarah R. Bowles,	2 " "	" Bassett.
Emma F. Burrill,	3 " "	" Harrington.
Rebecca J. Weston,	4 " "	" Bassett.
Deborah K. Burgess,	5 " "	" Drew.
Sarah Farley,	6 " "	" Lamb.
Eliza E. Foster,	7 " "	" Drew.
Mary Beal,	1 — Way Street,	" Manning.
Charlotte L. Young,	2 " "	" Ross.
Annie L. Pierce,	3 " "	" Manning.

CHAPMAN SCHOOL DISTRICT.

COMMITTEE.

Edwin Wright, *Chairman*, 134 Lexington Street.
Bradford L. Crocker, *Secretary*, 124 Webster Street.
J. Harvey Woodbury, 4 Princeton Street.
Samuel T. Cobb, 2 Belmont Square.
Seth C. Ames, 131 Webster Street.
Horace Dodd, 178 Salem Street.
Timothy H. Smith, 82 Salem Street.
Warren H. Cudworth, 1 Meridian Street.

M

CHAPMAN SCHOOL, EUTAW STREET.

John P. Averill, *Master*,
  Cl. I., Div. 1(

George R. Marble, *Sub-Master*,
  Cl. I., Div. 2.

James W. Webster, *Sub-Master*,
  Cl. II., Divs. 1 and 2.

Ellen R. White, *Head Assistant*,
  Cl. I., Div. 1.

Philura Wright, *Head Assistant*,
  Cl. IV., Div. 1.

Roxellana Howard, *Head Assistant*,
  Cl. II., Div. 1.

Maria D. Kimball, *Head Assistant*,
  Cl. II., Div. 1.

Assistants.

Sarah F. Russell,
  Cl. I., Div. 2.

Sarah E. Batcheller,
  Cl. II., Div. 2.

A. Delia Stickney,
  Cl. II., Div. 2.

Mary E. Moore,
  Cl. III., Div. 1.

Louisa M. Collyer,
  Cl. III., Div. 1.

Melissa E. D'Arcy,
  Cl. III., Divs. 1 and 2.

Sarah T. Butler,
  Cl. III., Div. 2.

Jane F. Reid,
  Cl. III., Div. 2.

Olive L. Rogers,
  Cl. IV., Divs. 1 and 2.

Ellen I. Bishop,
  Cl. IV., Div. 1.

Caroline Whitney,
  Cl. IV., Div. 2.

Lydia B. Smith,
  Cl. IV., Div. 2.

Ellen F. Ryder,
  Cl. IV., Div. 2.

Harriet N. Weed,
  Cl. IV., Div. 3.

Frances C. Close, *Teacher of Sewing.*
————— —————, *Teacher of Music.*

PRIMARY SCHOOLS.

Teachers.	Location.	Sub-Committee.
Ellenette Pillsbury,	No. 1 — Lexington Street,	⎫
Mary C. Hall,	2 " "	⎬ Mr. Wright.
Frances H. Turner,	3 " "	⎭
Hannah F. Crafts,	1 — Monmouth Street,	⎫ " Crocker.
Margaret A. Bartlett,	2 " "	⎭
Harriet N. Tyler,	1 — Bennington Hall,	" Wright.
Jane E. Beale,	1 — Porter Street,	⎫
Sarah A. Pratt,	2 " "	⎪
Mary D. Day,	3 " "	⎬ Messrs. Woodbury
M. Jane Peaslee,	4 " "	and Dodd.
Huldah H. Mitchell,	5 " "	⎪
Caroline A. Littlefield,	6 " "	⎭
Caroline L. Ditson,	1 — Saratoga Street, No. 224,	⎫
Almaretta J. Critchett,	2 " " "	⎬ Mr. Woodbury
Mary E. Gray,	3 " " "	⎭
Mary A. Ford,	1 " " No. 37	⎫ " "
Ellen M. Robbins,	2 " " "	⎭

DWIGHT SCHOOL DISTRICT.

COMMITTEE.

Mathias Rich, *Chairman*, 8 West Dedham Street.
Benjamin W. Williams, *Secretary*, 36 Clarendon Street.
William H. Learnard, Jr. 61 Rutland Street.
Joseph L. Drew, 52 Warren Street.
Alden Speare, 15 East Brookline Street.
M. Denman Ross, 76 Boylston Street.
Stephen L. Emery, 603 Tremont Street.
Charles W. Slack, 10 Garland Street.
Robert C. Waterston, 71 Chester Square.
Ira L. Moore, 650 Washington Street.

DWIGHT SCHOOL, SPRINGFIELD STREET.

James A. Page, *Master*,	Lucius A. Wheelock, *Usher*,
Cl. I., Div. 1.	Cl. II., Div. 1.
Charles Hutchins, *Sub-Master*,	Mary T. Ross, *Head Assistant*,
Cl. I., Div. 2.	Cl. I., Div. 1.

Assistants.

Mary C. Browne,	Jane M. Hight,
Cl. II., Div. 2,	Cl. III., Div. 4.
Martha A. Joslin,	Clara B. Gould,
Cl. III., Div. 1.	Cl. IV., Div. 1.
Eliza A. Allen,	S. Amelia Everett,
Cl. III., Div. 2.	Cl. IV., Div. 2.
Eva M. Keller,	Jane E. Bunton,
Cl. III., Div. 3.	Cl. IV., Div. 3.
	Sarah J. Pilsbury,
	Cl. IV., Div. 4.

Joseph B. Sharland, *Teacher of Music.*
Thomas W. Pemberton, *Janitor.*

PRIMARY SCHOOLS.

Teachers.	Location.		Sub-Committees.
Mary C. R. Towle,	No. 1 —	Rutland Street,	Mr. Waterston.
Martha B. Lucas,	2	" "	" Slack.
Sarah E. Crocker,	3	" "	" Rich.
Henrietta Draper,	4	" "	" Williams.
Eliza G. Swett,	5	" "	" Speare.
Jane P. Titcomb,	6	" "	" Moore.

ELIOT SCHOOL DISTRICT.

COMMITTEE.

Edward D. G. Palmer, *Chairman*, 3 Montgomery Place.
Joseph D. Fallon, *Secretary*, 47 Court Street.
Charles A. Turner, 364 Hanover Street.
George F. Haskins, 2 North Square.
Benjamin Fessenden, 25 Charter Street.
Benjamin T. Gould, 1 Prospect Street.
Horace Dodd, 178 Salem Street.
William A. Krueger, 42 Sheafe Street.
Warren S. Beal, 2 Blossom Court.
Michael Leary, Merrimac House.

ELIOT SCHOOL, NORTH BENNET STREET.

Samuel W. Mason, *Master*,
Cl. I., Div. 1.
McLaurin, F. Cook, *Sub-Master*,
Cl. I., Div. 2.

Walter H. Newell, *Usher*,
Cl. II., Div. 1.
Marcy Foster, *Head Assistant*,
Cl. I., Div. 1.

Assistants.

Elizabeth M. Turner,
Cl. II., Div. 2.
Sarah C. Goodrich,
Cl. II., Div. 3.
Mary A. E. Sargent,
Cl. III., Div. 1.
Frances M. Bodge,
Cl. III., Div. 2.
Sarah Larrabee,
Cl. III., Div. 3.

Mary F. Perkins,
Cl. III., Div. 4.
O. Augusta Welch,
Cl. IV., Div. 1.
Mary E. Hutchins,
Cl. IV., Div. 2.
Georgiana D. Russell,
Cl. IV., Div. 3.
Lydia K. Potter,
Cl. IV., Div. 4.

Joseph B. Sharland, *Music Teacher.*
Patrick Reardon, *Janitor.*

PRIMARY SCHOOLS.

Teachers.	Location.	Sub-Committees.
Sarah A. Winsor,	No. 1 — Snelling Place,	} Mr. Dodd.
Sophia Shepherd,	2 " "	
Clarissa Davis,	3 " "	" Fessenden.
Cleone G. Tewksbury,	4 " "	" Fallon.

Antonia Harvey,	5 — Snelling Place,	Mr. Palmer.
Harriet S. Boody,	6 " "	" Fessenden.
Eliza Brintnall,	1 — 22 Charter Street.	" Gould.
Eliza J. Cosgrave,	2 " "	" Turner.
———— ————,	3 " "	} " Leary.
Juliaette Davis,	4 " "	
Julia Ann Cutts,	1 — Rear 22 Charter Street,	" Turner.
Sarah Ripley,	2 " "	} " Beal.
Josephine O. Paine,	3 " "	
Frances E. Harrod,	1 — North Bennet Street,	" Krueger.
Catharine S. Sawyer,	2 " " "	" Palmer.
Mary E. Barrett,	3 " " "	" Haskins.
Margaret J. Flood,	4 " " "	" Gould.

EVERETT SCHOOL DISTRICT.

COMMITTEE.

Alden Speare, *Chairman*, 15 East Brookline Street.
Stephen L. Emery, *Secretary*, 603 Tremont Street.
Charles W. Slack, 10 Garland Street.
Matthias Rich, 8 West Dedham Street.
William H. Learnard, Jr. 61 Rutland Street.
Edmund T. Eastman, 50 Essex Street.
Charles H. Spring, 7 Harrison Avenue.
M. Denman Ross, 76 Boylston Street.
Robert C. Waterston, 71 Chester Square.
Benjamin W. Williams, 36 Clarendon Street.

EVERETT SCHOOL, WEST NORTHAMPTON STREET.

George B. Hyde, *Master*,
  Cl. I., Div. 1.
Francis E. Keller, *Head Assistant*,
  Cl. I., Div. 1.

Anna C. Ellis, *Head Assistant*,
  Cl. III., Div. 2.
Emma F. Titus, *Head Assistant*,
  Cl. I., Div. 3.
Louisa Tucker, *Head Assistant*,
  Cl. II., Div. 1.

Assistants.

Helen Beaumont,
  Cl. I., Div. 2.
Frances R. Josselyn,
  Cl. II., Div. 3.
Anna B. Thompson,
  Cl. II., Div. 3.
Emily F. Tolman,
  Cl. III., Div. 1.

Mary A. Gavett,
  Cl. III., Div. 3.
Louisa M. Alline,
  Cl. IV., Div. 1.
Elizabeth A. Browne,
  Cl. IV., Div. 2.
Ann J. Bolden,
  Cl. IV., Div. 3.
Sarah W. Pollard,
  Cl. IV., Div. 4.

Martha A. Sargent, *Teacher of Sewing.*
—————— ——————, *Music Teacher.*
Thomas W. Pemberton, *Janitor.*

PRIMARY SCHOOLS.

Teachers.	*Location.*	*Sub-Committees.*
Eliza C. Gould,	No. 1 — Concord Street,	Mr. Williams.
Laura A. Farnsworth,	2 " "	" Speare.
Mary A. Crocker,	3 " "	} " Slack.
Anna R. Frost,	4 " "	
Caroline S. Lamb,	5 " "	" Learnard.
Lydia A. Sawyer,	6 " "	" Spring.
Mary T. Bunton,	7 " "	" Eastman.
Hannah M. Coolidge,	9 " "	" Ross.
Caroline F. Barr,	11 " "	" Rich.
Lydia F. Blanchard,	12 " "	" Waterston.

FRANKLIN SCHOOL DISTRICT.

COMMITTEE.

Enoch C. Rolfe, *Chairman,* 616 Washington Street.
Benjamin W. Williams, *Secretary,* 36 Clarendon Street.
Ira L. Moore, 650 Washington Street.
William E. Underwood, 743 Washington Street.
William H. Learnard, Jr. 61 Rutland Street.
Matthias Rich, 8 West Dedham Street.
Alden Speare, 15 East Brookline Street.
Joseph L. Drew, 52 Warren Street.
Robert C. Waterston, 71 Chester Square.
Stephen L. Emery, 603 Tremont Street.
Charles W. Slack, 10 Garland Street.

FRANKLIN SCHOOL, RINGGOLD STREET.

Granville B. Putnam, *Master*,
Cl. I., Div. 1.
Amelia B. Hopkins, *Head Assistant*,
Cl. I., Div. 1.

Sarah A. Gale, *Head Assistant*,
Cl. I., Div. 2.
Sarah P. Mitchell, *Head Assistant*,
Cl. I., Div. 3.
Catharine T. Simonds, *Head Assistant*,
Cl. IV., Div. 1.

Assistants.

Lydia H. Emmons,
Cl. II., Div. 1.
Mary J. Leach,
Cl. II., Div. 2.
Isabella M. Harmon,
Cl. II., Div. 3.
Elizabeth J. Brown,
Cl. III., Div. 1.
L. Isabel Barry,
Cl. III., Div. 2.

P. Catharine Bradford,
Cl. III., Div. 3.
Abby D. Tucker,
Cl. III., Div. 4.
Anna E. Parker,
Cl. IV., Div. 2.
Mary A. Mitchell,
Cl. IV., Div. 3.
Susan E. Gates,
Cl. IV., Div. 4.

Maria S. Walcott, *Sewing Teacher.*
——— ———, *Music Teacher.*
Amos Lincoln, *Janitor.*

PRIMARY SCHOOLS.

Teachers.	Location.		Sub-Committees.
Lucy M. Beck,	No. 1 — Genesee Street,		Mr. Rolfe.
Susan H. Chaffee,	2	" "	" Drew.
Anna T. Corliss,	3	" "	" Slack.
Josephine G. Whipple,	1 — Suffolk Street,		" Underwood.
Georgiana A. Ballard,	2	" "	" Moore.
Frances M. Sylvester,	3	" "	" Underwood.
Hannah E. Perry,	4	" "	" Williams.
Maria Jenkins,	5	" "	" Slack.
Elizabeth P. Cummings,	6	" "	" Learnard.
Eliza J. Dyer,	7	" "	" Waterston.
Julia M. Brown,	8	" "	" Rolfe.
Harriet M. Faxon,	1 — Groton Street,		" Square.
Sarah S. Saunders,	2	" "	" Williams.
Frances J. Crocker,	3	" "	" Slack.
Sarah F. Mason,	4	" "	" Moore.
Lucy A. Cate,	5	" "	" Rich.
Caroline A. Miller,	6	" "	" Learnard.

HANCOCK SCHOOL DISTRICT.

COMMITTEE.

Charles A. Turner, *Chairman*, 364 Hanover Street.
Joseph D. Fallon, *Secretary*, 47 Court Street.
E. D. G. Palmer, 3 Montgomery Place.
George F. Haskins, 2 North Square.
Aaron P. Richardson, 17 Green Street.
Benjamin Fessenden, 25 Charter Street.
Horace Dodd, 178 Salem Street.
George Hubbard, 3½ Portland Street.
Dexter S. King, 34 Bowdoin Street.
William A. Krueger, 42 Sheafe Street.
Timothy H. Smith, 82 Salem Street.

HANCOCK SCHOOL, RICHMOND PLACE.

William E. Sheldon, *Master.*
  Cl. I., Div. 1.
Angelina A. Brigham, *Head Assistant.*
  Cl. I., Div. 1.

Mary L. Sheffield, *Head Assistant.*
  Cl. I., Div. 2.

Assistants.

Alicia H. Gilley,
  Cl. I., Div. 3.
Amy E. Bradford,
  Cl. I., Div. 2.
Helen M. Hitchins,
  Cl. II., Div. 1.
Josephine M. Robertson,
  Cl. II., Div. 2.
Emily F. Fessenden,
  Cl. II., Div. 3.
Martha F. Winning,
  Cl. II., Div. 4.
Ellen A. Hunt,
  Cl. III., Div. 1.
Mary Carleton,
  Cl. III., Div. 2.

Sarah E. White,
  Cl. III., Div. 3.
Sarah F. Stevens,
  Cl. III., Div. 4.
Kate S. Doane,
  Cl. IV., Div. 1.
Henrietta L. Pierce,
  Cl. IV., Div. 2.
Achsah Barnes,
  Cl. IV., Div. 3.
Malvina R. Brigham,
  Cl. IV., Div. 4.
Augusta C. Kimball,
  Cl. IV., Div. 5.
Mary E. Nichols.

Caroline Z. Harrod, *Teacher of Sewing.*
Joseph B. Sharland, *Teacher of Music.*
Franklin Eveleth, *Janitor.*

PRIMARY SCHOOLS.

Teachers.	Location.	Sub-Committees.
Sarah J. Copp,	No. 1 — Thacher Street,	Mr. Richardson.
M. Alice Mansfield,	2 " "	" Turner.
Sarah L. Shepherd,	3 " "	" Hubbard.
Mary S. Gale,	1 — North Margin Street,	" Dodd.
Mary J. Clark,	2 " "	" Palmer.
Mary P. Taylor,	1 — Hanover Street,	} " Fallon.
Emily A. Tewksbury,	2 " "	
Mary C. Hayden.	3 " "	" Krueger.
Adeline S. Bodge,	1 — Bennet Avenue,	" King.
Ellen C. Sawtelle,	2 " "	" Fessenden.
Esther W. Mansfield,	1 — Sheafe Street,	" "
Eunice F. Linsley,	2 " "	" Turner.
Martha F. Boody,	3 " "	" Richardson.
Susan Page,	2 — Cooper Street,	} " Smith.
Harriet B. Vose,	3 " "	
Sarah F. Ellis,	4 " "	" Dodd.
Mary E. Gallagher,	1 — Hanover Avenue,	" Haskins.
Augusta H. Barrett,	2 " "	" Fessenden.
Maria A. Gibbs,	3 " "	" Haskins.

LAWRENCE SCHOOL DISTRICT.

COMMITTEE.

Edward H. Brainard, *Chairman*, 161 Broadway.
Nathaniel Hayes, *Secretary*, E Street, Cor. Broadway.
J. Proctor Haskins, 8 Woodward Street.
Edwin Briggs, 67 Dorchester Street.
Francis H. Underwood, 282 Fourth Street.
Henry A. Drake, 333 Broadway.
Charles H. Spring, 7 Harrison Avenue.
Michael Moran, 73 Purchase Street.

LAWRENCE SCHOOL, B STREET, SOUTH BOSTON.

Josiah A. Stearns, *Master,*
Cl. I., Div. 1.
Henry C. Hardon, *Sub-Master,*
Cl. I., Div. 2.

Margaret Kyle, *Head Assistant,*
Cl. I., Div. 1.
Mary W. Conant, *Head Assistant,*
Cl. II., Div. 1.
Kate W. Towne, *Head Assistant,*
Cl. II., Div. 2.

Assistants.

Juliette Smith,
Cl. II., Div. 3.
Alice Cooper,
Cl. II., Div. 4.
Martha A. Thompson,
Cl. III., Div. 1.
Sarah O. Babcock,
Cl. III., Div. 2.
Elizabeth S. Jefferds,
Cl. III., Div. 3.
Margarette A. Moody,
Cl. III., Div. 4.

Louisa C. Richards,
Cl. IV., Div. 1.
Margaret A. Gleason,
Cl. IV., Div. 2.
Caroline Blanchard,
Cl. IV., Div. 3.
Eliza L. Darling,
Cl. IV., Div. 4.
Mary N. Moses,
Cl. IV., Divs. 3 & 4.

Sarah J. Bliss, *Teacher of Sewing.*
Joseph B. Sharland, *Teacher of Music.*
J. C. Burton, *Janitor.*

PRIMARY SCHOOLS.

Teachers.	*Location.*		*Sub-Committees.*
Lucinda Smith,	No. 1 — Silver Street,		
Sarah M. Dawson,	2 " "		Messrs. Spring and Moran.
Mary F. Peeler,	3 " "		
Sarah S. Blake,	4 " "		
Mary F. Baker,	5 " "		Messrs. Moran and Spring.
Mary A. Macnair,	6 " "		
Olive W. Green,	1 — Mather Schoolhouse,		Hayes & Underwood.
Mary E. Fox,	2 " "		Haskins and Hayes.
Sarah V. Cunningham,	3 " "		Hayes & Underwood.
Sarah F. Hall,	4 " "		
Mary K. Davis,	5 " "		Haskins and Hayes.
Mary Kyle,	6 " "		
Ann E. Newell,	7 " "		Hayes and Underwood.
Rebecca H. Bird,	8 " "		
Laura A. Reed,	9 " "		Briggs and Drake.
Mary Lincoln,	10 " "		

LINCOLN SCHOOL DISTRICT.

COMMITTEE.

Francis H. Underwood, *Chairman*, 282 Fourth Street.
Nathaniel Hayes, *Secretary*, E Street, corner of Broadway.
J. Proctor Haskins, 8 Woodward Street.
Henry A. Drake, 333 Broadway.
Edwin Briggs, 67 Dorchester Street.
Edward H. Brainard, 161 Broadway.
Charles Torrey, 105 Boylston Street.

LINCOLN SCHOOL, BROADWAY, SOUTH BOSTON.

Samuel Barrett, *Master*,
   Cl. I., Div. 1.
Charles A. Morrill, *Sub-Master*,
   Cl. I., Div. 2.

Mary E. Balch, *Head Assistant*,
   Cl. I., Div. 1.
Abby M. Holder, *Head Assistant*,
   Cl. II., Div. 1.
Myra S. Butterfield, *Head Assistant*.
   Cl. III., Div. 2.

Assistants.

Anne M. Brown,
   Cl. II., Div. 2.
Laura Bartlett,
   Cl. III., Div. 1.
Cynthia H. Sears,
   Cl. III., Div. 3.
Ariadne B. Jewell,
   Cl. IV., Div. 1.

Frances A. Nickles,
   Cl. IV., Div. 2.
Harriet A. Stowell,
   Cl. IV., Div. 3,
Ellen R. Wyman,
   Cl. IV., Div. 4.
Lucy W. Clark,
   Cl. IV., Div. 5.

Joseph B. Sharland, *Teacher of Vocal Music.*
Elizabeth Bedlington, *Teacher of Sewing.*
Melzar Stetson, *Janitor.*

PRIMARY SCHOOLS.

Teachers.	*Location.*	*Sub-Committees.*
Laura J. Gerry,	No. 3 — Lincoln Schoolhouse,	Torrey and Brainard.
Sarah E. Varney,	2 — Rear of Hawes Hall,	Haskins and Brainard.
Lucy C. Bartlett,	3 — Hawes Hall,	Page and Brainard.

Teachers.	Location.	Sub-Committees.
Caroline R. Holway,	1 — City Point,	
Caroline M. Lyon,	2 " "	
Tiley A. Bolkcom,	3 " "	Hayes and Drake.
Susan W. Smith,	4 " "	
Mary H. Faxon,	" " Chapel,	Torrey and Brainard
Mary E. Easton,	" " "	

LYMAN SCHOOL DISTRICT.

COMMITTEE.

J. Harvey Woodbury, *Chairman*, 4 Princeton Street.
Warren H. Cudworth, *Secretary*, 1 Meridian Street.
Bradford L. Crocker, 124 Webster Street.
Samuel T. Cobb, 2 Belmont Square.
Seth C. Ames, 131 Webster Street.
George Hubbard, 3½ Portland Street.
Edwin Wright, 134 Lexington Street.

LYMAN SCHOOL, MERIDIAN STREET, EAST BOSTON.

Hosea H. Lincoln, *Master*,
   Cl. I., Div. 1.
James F. Blackinton, *Sub-Master*,
   Cl. II.

Emma Clark, *Head Assistant*,
   Cl. I., Div. 2.
Cordelia Lothrop, *Head Assistant*,
   Cls. II. and III.
Eliza F. Russell, *Head Assistant*,
   Cl. III.

Assistants.

Mary A. Turner,
   Cl. IV., Div. 1.
Amelia H. Pitman,
   Cl. IV., Div. 1.

Harriet N. Webster,
   Cl. IV., Div. 1.
Lucy J. Lothrop,
   Cl. IV., Div. 2.

Frances C. Close, *Teacher of Sewing.*
——— ———. *Teacher of Music.*

PRIMARY SCHOOLS.

Teachers.	Location.	Sub-Committees.
Anna J. Duncan,	No. 1 — Paris Street,	
Abby M. Allen,	2 " "	
Isabella A. Bilby,	3 " "	
Hannah C. Atkins,	4 " "	Cudworth and Hubbard.
*Susan H. M. Swan,	5 " "	
Hannah L. Manson,	6 " "	
Caroline S. Litchfield,	Ward Room,	
Angeline M. Cudworth,	Sumner Hall,	Mr. Crocker.
Jane P. Wood,	8 Elbow Street,	

MAYHEW SCHOOL DISTRICT.

COMMITTEE.

Samuel H. Winkley, *Chairman*, 5 Chambers Street.
Timothy H. Smith, *Secretary*, 82 Salem Street.
George Hubbard, 3½ Portland Street.
Dexter S. King, 34 Bowdoin Street.
William C. Williamson, 23 McLean Street.
Calvin G. Page, 69 Myrtle Street.
Orrin S. Sanders, 11 Bowdoin Street.

MAYHEW SCHOOL, HAWKINS STREET.

Samuel Swan, *Master*, and *Teacher of Music*, Cl. I., Div. 1.

L. Hall Grandgent, *Usher*, Cl. II., Div. 1.

Quincy E. Dickerman, *Sub-Master*, Cl. I., Div. 2.

Emily A. Moulton, *Head Assistant*, Cl. I., Div. 1.

Assistants.

Elizabeth P. Hopkins, Cl. II., Div. 2.
Sarah W. I. Copeland, Cl. III., Div. 1.
Caroline F. Reed, Cl. III., Div. 2.
Elizabeth L. West, Cl. III., Div. 3.

Florena Gray, Cl. IV., Div. 1.
Margaret R. Atkinson, Cl. IV., Div. 2.
Adeline F. Cutter, Cl. IV., Div. 3.

PRIMARY SCHOOLS.

Teachers.	*Location.*	*Sub-Committees.*
Sarah E. Copeland,	No. 1 — Chardon Street,	Mr. King.
Maria L. Cummings,	2 " "	" Sanders.
Bethiah Whiting,	3 " "	" Page.
Henrietta B. Tower,	5 " "	" Smith.
Permelia Stevens,	6 " "	" Sanders.
Delia F. Lindsley,	Old Hancock Schoolhouse,	" Smith.
Harriet S. Lothrop,	" "	} " Hubbard.
Harriet A. Farrow,	" "	
Lois M. Rea,	South Margin Street,	" Williamson.
Martha E. Lauriat,	67 Merrimac Street,	" Smith.

PHILLIPS SCHOOL DISTRICT.

COMMITTEE.

Loring Lothrop, *Chairman*, 43 Pinckney Street.
Henry Warren, *Secretary*, 25 Green Street.
J. Baxter Upham, 31 Chestnut Street.
S. K. Lothrop, 12 Chestnut Street.
John F. Jarvis, 22 Leverett Street.
Dexter S. King, 34 Bowdoin Street.
Henry Burroughs, Jr., 82 Mount Vernon Street.
Robert I. Burbank, 8 Staniford Street.

PHILLIPS SCHOOL, SOUTHAC STREET.

James Hovey, *Master*,
    Cl. I., Div. 1.
Amphion Gates, *Sub-Master*,
    Cl. I., Div. 2.

Elias H. Marston, *Usher*,
    Cl. II., Div. 1.
Emma J. Fuller, *Head Assistant*,
    Cl. I., Div. 1.

Assistants.

Laura M. Porter,	Hannah M. Sutton,
Cl. II., Div. 2.	Cl. IV., Div. 1.
Lucy S. Nevins,	Georgiana H. Moore,
Cl. II., Div. 1,	Cl. IV., Div. 2.
Abby A. Reed,	M. Josephine Dugan,
Cl. III., Div. 2.	Cl. IV., Div. 3.
Elvira M. Harrington,	Emily A. Perkins,
Cl. III., Div. 3.	Cl. IV., Div. 4.

Joseph B. Sharland, *Music Teacher.*

PRIMARY SCHOOLS.

Teachers.	Location.	Sub-Committees.
Caroline P. Eastman,	No. 1 — Southac Street,	Mr. Jarvis.
Sarah A. M. Turner,	2 " "	" Warren
Mary A. Allen,	3 " "	" Burbank.
Eliza A. Corthell,	1 — Old Phillips Schoolhouse,	" Jarvis.
Sarah Ingalls,	2 " " "	
Emeline D. Fish,	3 " " "	} " King.
Harriet H. King,	1 — Joy Street,	
Ruth M. Sanborn,	Western Avenue,	" Upham.
Addie L. Jepson,	Phillips Schoolhouse,	" Warren.

QUINCY SCHOOL DISTRICT.

COMMITTEE.

Charles Torrey, *Chairman*, 105 Boylston Street.
Edmund T. Eastman, *Secretary*, 50 Essex Street.
Henry W. Harrington, 3 Corey Avenue.
William E. Underwood, 743 Washington Street.
Thomas M. Brewer, 8 Edinboro' Street.
Elijah C. Drew, 40 State Street.
Patrick Riley, 10 Lincoln Street.
George Hayward, 13 Temple Place.
William H. Page, 48 Beach Street.
Charles Butler, 291 Washington Street.
Ira L. Moore, 650 Washington Street.

QUINCY SCHOOL, TYLER STREET.

Charles E. Valentine, *Master*,
   Cl. I., Div. 1.
E. Frank Wood, *Sub-Master*,
   Cl. I., Div. 2.
Henry C. Bullard, *Usher*,
   Cl. II., Div. 1.

Annie M. Lund, *Head Assistant*,
   Cl. I., Div. 1.
Lydia A. Hanson, *Head Assistant*,
   Cl. II., Div. 2.

Assistants.

Harriet D. Hinckley,
   Cl. II., Div. 3.
Louisa F. Monroe,
   Cl. III., Div. 1.
Angeline A. Moulton,
   Cl. III., Div. 2.
Emily J. Tucker,
   Cl. III., Div. 3.
Olive M. Page,
   Cl. III., Div. 4.

——————,
   Cl. IV., Div, 1.
Elizabeth T. Bailey,
   Cl. IV., Div. 2.
Charlotte L. Wheelwright,
   Cl. IV., Div. 3.
Emily B. Peck,
   Cl. IV., Div. 4.
Anna F. Hinckley,
   Cl. IV., Div. 5.

Joseph B. Sharland, *Teacher of Music.*
Daniel Keefe, *Janitor.*

BRANCH OF QUINCY SCHOOL.

OLD FRANKLIN SCHOOLHOUSE.

Alfred Bunker, *Usher*,
   Cl. II., Div. 3.

E. Maria Simonds, *Head Assistant*,
   Cl. III., Div. 2.

Assistants.

Mary A. Sylvester,
   Cl. III., Div. 4.
Emma M. Thomas,
   Cl. IV., Div. 2.

——————————,
   Cl. IV., Div. 4.

PRIMARY SCHOOLS.

Teachers.	Location.			Sub-Committers.
Susan Frizzell,	No. 1 — East Street.			Mr. Moore.
Elizabeth P. Bentley,	2	"	"	" Harrington.
Mary L. Richards,	3	"	"	" Hayward.
Caroline D. Pollard,	4	"	"	" Underwood.
Dora Norton,	5	"	"	" Moore.
Ellen E. Leach,	6	"	"	" Butler.
Catharine R. Greenwood.	7	"	"	" Drew.
Abby F. Hutchins,	8	"	"	" Brewer.
Harriet A. Bettis,	9	"	"	" Page.
Priscilla Johnson,	10	"	"	
Sarah E. Lewis,	11	"	"	} " Eastman.
Elizabeth C. Frink,	12	"	"	" Brewer.
Sophronia N. Herrick.	1	"	"	Place. " Drew.
Marian A. Flynn,	2	"	"	" " Riley.
Hannah A. Lawrence,	3	"	"	"
Adeline Stockbridge,	4	"	"	" } " Torrey.
Matilda Mitchell,	Engine House, East Street,			" Harrington.

WELLS SCHOOL DISTRICT.

COMMITTEE.

John F. Jarvis, *Chairman*, 22 Leverett Street.
Henry Warren, *Secretary*, 25 Green Street.
Benjamin T. Gould, 1 Prospect Street.
Loring Lothrop, 43 Pinckney Street.
Samuel H. Winkley, 5 Chambers Street.
Aurelius L. Weymouth, 9 Green Street.
Michael Leary, Merrimac House.
William C. Williamson, 23 McLean Street.
Warren S. Beal, 2 Blossom Court.

WELLS SCHOOL, BLOSSOM STREET.

Reuben Swan, *Master*,	Sarah J. Sanborn, *Head Assistant*.
Cl. I., Div. 1.	Cl. I., Div. 2.
Ellen F. Preble, *Head Assistant*.	Bessie T. Capen, *Head Assistant*.
Cl. I., Div. 1.	Cl. I., Div. 2.

N

Assistants.

Mary S. Carter,
     Cl. II., Div. 1.
Sarah J. Lothrop,
     Cl. II., Div. 2.
Juliana Sparrell,
     Cl. III., Div. 1.
Lydia S. Chandler,
     Cl. III., Div. 2.

Ellen M. Brown,
     Cl. IV., Div. 1.
Lydia A. Beck,
     Cl. IV., Div. 2.
Elizabeth P. Winning,
     Cl. IV., Div. 2.
Matilda A. Gerry,
     Cl. IV., Div. 3.

Joseph B. Sharland, *Teacher of Music.*
James Martin, *Janitor.*

PRIMARY SCHOOLS.

Teachers.	Location.	Sub-Committees.
Elizabeth D. McCluer,	No. 1 — Wall Street,	} Mr. Warren.
Mary F. Jones,	2 " "	
Anna A. James,	3 " "	" Gould.
Sarah A. Randall,	4 " "	} " Winkley.
Harriet O. Brown,	5 " "	
Mary L. Bailey,	6 " "	" Leary.
Lucy M. A. Redding,	1 — Poplar Street,	" Lothrop.
Maria W. Turner,	2 " "	" Weymouth.
Elizabeth W. Snow,	3 " "	} " Beal.
Sarah C. Chevaillier,	4 " "	
Elizabeth S. Foster,	5 " "	" Weymouth.
Mary S. Watts,	6 " "	" Williamson.

WINTHROP SCHOOL DISTRICT.

COMMITTEE.

Thomas M. Brewer, *Chairman*, 8 Edinboro' Street.
Salem T. Lamb, *Secretary*, 10 Burroughs Place.
Elisha Bassett, 335 Tremont Street.
Elijah C. Drew, 40 State Street.
Ezra Palmer, 1 Tremont Place.
Enoch C. Rolfe, 616 Washington Street.

Charles Edward Cook, 220 Washington Street.
Charles H. Spring, 7 Harrison Avenue.
Jacob M. Manning, 9 Boylston Place.
William H. Page, 48 Beach Street.

WINTHROP SCHOOL, TREMONT STREET.

Robert Swan, *Master.* Rebecca P. Barry, *Head Assistant,*
Cl. I., Div. 3.
Susan A. W. Loring, *Head Assistant,* Almira Seymour, *Head Assistant,*
Cl. I., Div. 1. Cl. II., Div. 1.
May Gertrude Ladd, *Head Assistant,* Mary Newell, *Head Assistant,*
Cl. I., Div. 2. Cl. II., Div. 2.

Assistants.

Abbie A. Cutter, Mary J. Danforth,
Cl. I., Div. 1. Cl. III., Div. 3.
Maria L. S. Ogden, Julia A. Jellison,
Cl. II., Div. 3. Cl. III., Div. 4.
Mary E. Moorhouse, Emma K. Valentine,
Cl. II., Div. 3. Cl. IV., Div. 1.
Elizabeth S. Emmons, Frances C. Jennison,
Cl. III., Div. 1. Cl. IV., Div. 2.
Mary E. Davis, Hannah H. Hosmer,
Cl. III., Div. 1. Cl. IV., Div. 3.
Narcissa A. Avery, Emily M. Hathaway,
Cl. III., Div. 2. Cl. IV., Div. 4.

Hannah A Rolfe, *Teacher of Sewing.*
—————— ————, *Teacher of Music.*
Daniel O'Keefe, *Janitor.*

PRIMARY SCHOOLS.

Teachers.	*Location.*	*Sub-Committees.*
Ella M. Seaverns,	No. 1 — Harrison Avenue,	Mr. Page.
Rebecca R. Thayer,	2 " "	" Palmer.
Abby M. Mills,	3 " "	" Brewer.
Mary B. Brown,	4 " "	" Rolfe.
Mary A. B. Gore,	1 — Tyler Street,	" Drew.
Anna O. Jones,	2 " "	" Manning.
Abby J. Glover,	3 " "	" Brewer.

Teachers.	Location.	Sub-Committees.
Caroline M. Grover,	No. 4 — Tyler Street,	} Mr. Cook.
Hannah E. Moore,	5 " "	
Frances Torrey,	6 " "	" Spring.
Anna M. Penniman,	1 — Hudson Street,	} " Bassett.
Caroline L. P. Torrey,	2 " "	
Agnes Duncan,	3 " "	} " Lamb.
Henrietta K. Madigan,	4 " "	

TRUANT OFFICERS.

The city is divided into four Truant Districts, each comprehending five school districts, as shown in the following table : —

OFFICERS.	DISTRICTS.	SCHOOL DISTRICTS BELONGING.
Chase Cole,	North,	Adams, Chapman, Eliot, Hancock, Lyman.
George M. Felch,	Central,	Boylston, Bowdoin, Mayhew, Phillips, Wells.
E. G. Richardson,	Southern,	Brimmer, Bowditch, Franklin, Quincy, Winthrop.
Phineas Bates.	South,	Bigelow, Dwight, Everett, Lawrence, Lincoln.

Each officer has order-boxes at certain convenient places in his district, where teachers may send notes when they desire to report cases of truancy to him.

These boxes are located as follows : —

ORDER-BOXES.

North District.

Police Station No. 1, Hanover Street.
Police Station No. 8, East Boston.

Central District.

Boylston School, Mayhew School.
Police Station No. 3, Joy Street.

Southern District.

Corner of Harrison Avenue and Castle Street.
Police Station No. 4, East Dedham Street.
Corner of South and Summer streets.
Nos. 228 and 306 Tremont Street.

South District.

Police Station No. 4, East Dedham Street.
Police Station No. 6, South Boston.

All the Truant Officers meet every Monday morning at 10½ o'clock at the Truant Court Room, in the Court House, Court Square. Also at 12 o'clock on the first Monday of each month, at the room of the Superintendent of Schools.

www.ingramcontent.com/pod-product-compliance
Lightning Source LLC
Chambersburg PA
CBHW030629270326
41927CB00007B/1359